Cambridge Elements

Elements in Global Development Studies
edited by
Peter Ho
Zhejiang University
Servaas Storm
Delft University of Technology

DEVELOPMENT SUBJECTIVITIES, GOVERNMENTALITY, AND MIGRATION MANAGEMENT IN THE PACIFIC

Lya Mainé Astonitas
The University of Auckland

Shaftesbury Road, Cambridge CB2 8EA, United Kingdom

One Liberty Plaza, 20th Floor, New York, NY 10006, USA

477 Williamstown Road, Port Melbourne, VIC 3207, Australia

314–321, 3rd Floor, Plot 3, Splendor Forum, Jasola District Centre, New Delhi – 110025, India

103 Penang Road, #05–06/07, Visioncrest Commercial, Singapore 238467

Cambridge University Press is part of Cambridge University Press & Assessment, a department of the University of Cambridge.

We share the University's mission to contribute to society through the pursuit of education, learning and research at the highest international levels of excellence.

www.cambridge.org
Information on this title: www.cambridge.org/9781009462648

DOI: 10.1017/9781009400213

© Lya Mainé Astonitas 2024

This publication is in copyright. Subject to statutory exception and to the provisions of relevant collective licensing agreements, no reproduction of any part may take place without the written permission of Cambridge University Press & Assessment.

When citing this work, please include a reference to the DOI 10.1017/9781009400213

First published 2024

A catalogue record for this publication is available from the British Library.

ISBN 978-1-009-46264-8 Hardback
ISBN 978-1-009-40025-1 Paperback
ISSN 2634-0313 (online)
ISSN 2634-0305 (print)

Cambridge University Press & Assessment has no responsibility for the persistence or accuracy of URLs for external or third-party internet websites referred to in this publication and does not guarantee that any content on such websites is, or will remain, accurate or appropriate.

Development Subjectivities, Governmentality, and Migration Management in the Pacific

Elements in Global Development Studies

DOI: 10.1017/9781009400213
First published online: December 2024

Lya Mainé Astonitas
The University of Auckland

Author for correspondence: Lya Mainé Astonitas, last303@aucklanduni.ac.nz

Abstract: To advance the debates around temporary migration in the Pacific, a governmentality framework contributes to understanding social and historical relations produced by migration management at regional, country, and individual scales. The Recognised Seasonal Employer's (RSE) scheme, the Pacific epitome of regulated migration, temporarily recruits participants from labour-rich countries to work in New Zealand's horticulture and viticulture sectors. Driven by agricultural labour shortfalls, it was conceived and promoted as a development intervention for Pacific countries, and is regularly claimed to provide a 'triple win' for employers and industry, in Pacific countries via remittances, and participants' communities. Missing from these claims is an understanding of how seasonal migration fits into new migration management regimes, and the instruments deployed to enable this omission. To appreciate how workers' subjectivities are transformed to favour labour mobility, the spotlight is on the scheme's articulation as a development instrument, its operationalisation, and the mundane day-to-day situations it entails.

This Element also has a video abstract: www.cambridge.org/EGDS_Astonitas

Keywords: seasonal agricultural labour, temporary labour migration, governmentality and subjectivities, guestworkers in commercial agriculture, government-managed migration

© Lya Mainé Astonitas 2024

ISBNs: 9781009462648 (HB), 9781009400251 (PB), 9781009400213 (OC)
ISSNs: 2634-0313 (online), 2634-0305 (print)

Contents

1 Introduction: Migration and Development from a Governmentality Framework   1

2 Contextualising the Recognised Seasonal Employer's Scheme in the Pacific   14

3 Governmentality in the RSE Scheme   27

4 Winners and Losers: Transforming Subjectivities   37

5 Conclusions   56

References   61

1 Introduction: Migration and Development from a Governmentality Framework

Across the world, year after year, several hundred thousand migrants participate in seasonal agricultural migration programmes, about 600,000 of them temporarily travelling to OECD countries. This increases migrants' reliance on foreign income as well as that of high-income countries on agricultural workers from middle- and low-income countries. Temporary migration for work is not a new phenomenon. Nonetheless, there has been a change in paradigm from the post-World War II guest worker programmes to the current ones. In parallel to the international 2000s' debate regarding the so-called migration-development nexus, a new generation of circular migration programmes was developed, so that by the mid-2000s, almost all OECD countries had them in place (OECD, 2008). This resurgence of temporary migration programmes was justified as a way of preventing irregular migration and security incidents, under the assumption that the promotion of regulated options would discourage the use of non-regulated channels for migration.

Governments in the Pacific region have consistently expressed their interest in migration and development, as over the last six decades citizens have moved in various ways between their home countries and the more developed economies of New Zealand and Australia. In the early pre- and post-independent Pacific period, colonial processes still heavily influenced forms of mobility. Migration for work and education was encouraged in the Pacific, as education systems were nascent and there were limited employment opportunities. Despite significant investment in education systems in the Pacific, decades later, migration for education and work continues. Many Pacific countries government leaders are educated in New Zealand and Australia. Expectations that future leaders require education abroad remain, and intergenerational aspirations for better prospects prevail.

Over this same time, many Pacific citizens took different opportunities to travel and live in the wealthier countries in the Pacific and beyond, where they could earn higher incomes. Employed mostly as semi-skilled workers, their steady remittances are welcome in their home countries, even as the prospect of them returning becomes an increasingly distant plan. In the last decade and a half, another flow of Pacific citizens has emerged, those who have the opportunity to undertake short term, seasonal agricultural work, in New Zealand and Australia, from where they remit or return home with significant resources. This change in migration patterns is the manifestation of a global shift in development policy, by which migration is seen as essential for economic growth in both sending and receiving countries. In the Pacific region, these transnational flows are named labour mobility, a denomination which signals the spatial mobility of workers and their labour as a production factor.

Pacific people move to and from New Zealand and Australia in this and various other ways, yet the predominant analytical approach used in migration and development literature, and especially in development economics, is that of push-pull theories. An alternative way to make sense of the contemporary dynamics of Pacific mobility is to situate contemporary practices, in a historical trajectory that makes explicit connections to colonial practices of governing and managing people in the Pacific. The rationalities, strategies, and day-to-day practices engendered by a particular migration management policy, the Recognised Seasonal Employer's (RSE) scheme, are analysed from a relational approach using a governmentality framework and with insights from fieldwork in New Zealand and Vanuatu. A broader timeframe is provided to understand the intransigence generated by entangled colonial power relations, how they collide and merge with traditional – customary – worldviews, and how these ensure the continuation of the RSE scheme. Due to the negligible international migration Vanuatu had before the scheme became available (Hayes, 2010), this case study, facilitates analysing how the rationale of development influences ni-Vanuatu engagement with the scheme. Nonetheless, similarities can be found with other Pacific participants and temporary migrant workers elsewhere.

Drawing on the Foucauldian concept of governmentality, as appropriated by Rose (1999, 2000), Lemke (2001, 2007, 2011), and Geiger and Pécoud (2010), allows to explain how the rationale of attending to the welfare of populations through development narratives, underpins the promotion of seasonal labour migration, and particularly, the RSE scheme portrayal as a development programme. By examining the power differences in a range of social relations, among persons and institutions, an explicit relational approach to understanding the persistence of transnational flows is unfolded. Governmentality, as a relational approach, acknowledges that individuals stand in a range of relational positions, which are produced by historical experiences with others, peers, authority figures, and more formal institutions. Relations are dynamic, as individual and group behaviours are transformed through a variety of instruments. These instruments or governmental technologies, versions of which have governed Pacific mobility over time, are produced by certain modes of problematisation. The linkages among unemployment, the potential for insecurity, and the dependency of Pacific countries on external aid – common problematics ascribed to the region – transform ni-Vanuatu participants and their communities through their engagement in the RSE scheme.

Against this backdrop, these concepts and their application are examined using different scales of analysis. In the Introduction, the coupling of migration and development in policy-making within the management of temporary migration is explained, outlining the global trajectory of migration management and its governance to describe its underpinnings; including the 'triple win' narrative ascribed to it. This section develops key concepts behind the governmentality framework, the rationale for the focus on Vanuatu as a case study and the methods used. In the second section, after providing a brief historical overview of labour mobility in the Pacific region and the context that led to the uptake of the RSE scheme, a regional scale of analysis draws attention to the roles of different actors and to how the lack of labour in New Zealand's agricultural sector and of waged employment in Pacific countries were articulated to respond to governments' and private sector needs. That section concludes setting the framework for the new social relations established by the operationalisation of the RSE scheme and its coupling of labour mobility with development narratives.

The third section explains the different features of the RSE scheme using a governmentality framework. This understanding of how the social and political context of temporary transnational migration is produced by power relations is linked to the pre and post-colonial history of New Zealand and other countries in the South Pacific. The focus is on particular governmentality techniques used by epistemic communities driving the implementation of the RSE scheme, which are based on long-standing relations between Pacific countries and New Zealand. While this analysis focuses on the conceptualisation of the problems at a policy level, the fourth section delves into the lived experiences of RSE participants. By bringing attention to an individual scale, the transformations in the participants' subjectivities are evidenced, analysing how individuals have become RSE workers after complex negotiations with themselves and with the managers of labour mobility. Finally, the conclusions argue that the RSE scheme is symptomatic of the widely accepted development model for Pacific countries and their purported transition from semi-subsistence, non-capitalistic economies to neoliberal states. Widely shared problematisations and solutions conceptualise poverty and unemployment as a predicament of individuals, made responsible to solve them, sometimes capitalising on their own cultural values to become productive subjects.

1.1 The International Governance of Migration Management

Migration management conceptualises migration as a human phenomenon but at the same time problematises irregular migration. Workers, who are the cornerstone of migration management, are made responsible for achieving their own development by becoming a productive migrant/labour unit in the recipient economies. Beyond economic development and capital accumulation, migrants are also expected to enhance their human capital. Thus, the different mechanisms that migration management invokes to regulate the movement of people across borders, are used as tools against the lack of development in sending countries, and are expected to revert, at least to some extent, some of the conditions that initially motivated migration, such as poverty or unemployment. In this way, the developmental state (Adamson, Tsourapas, 2020) transforms individuals, institutions, and governments. Development becomes part of an apparatus of global governance aimed at managing risks and governing unruly populations (de Vries, 2007) through a range of governmental technologies including the securitisation of unstable areas, imagined as spaces of breakdown and in need of re-ordering (Duffield, 2001). Securitisation against sociocultural backwardness problematises the circulation of certain 'cultural types' in receiving countries (Duffield, 2006). Therefore, migration management signals the emergence of interconnected policy agendas related to migration, development, and security.

Demographic profiles are the main criteria used for the management of temporary migration. The surplus of working aged people in one country is linked to the deficit of workers in another. In economic terms, seasonal migration responds to the imperatives of sending and receiving countries, in ways that do not threaten local unskilled workers (Kalm, 2010). In practice, insights derived from the data produced through the management of migration programmes, are used to incrementally redefine and resolve problems, such as unemployment, cost of remittances, lack of entrepreneurial skills, among others. This signals that problematisation is not static but allows for the adjustment of concepts and objects' definitions. Once a new problem is identified, a new solution follows, as it is always assumed that situations can be more efficiently managed, giving way to an eternal optimism to manage problems (Miller, Rose, 2008). This speaks to the appetite to identify successes and failures of existing policies through periodic evaluations, a salient characteristic of the new public management approach at the core of migration management. It follows that migration can benefit all actors involved if experts' recommendations are fulfilled, as a given reality is considered programmable. Experts' knowledge is presented as technical and 'apolitical' and often intentionally using broad terms and definitions that allow for the discretion of government officials and other stakeholders responsible for course correction.

Across receiving countries and in alignment with the new public management agenda, by which the public sector is encouraged to develop a manager–client relationship with its citizens; migration management implies the enactment of a business-like model. Public policies are based on estimations of costs and benefits which target efficiency improvements through the appropriation of private sector management models. The adoption of migration management, with its 'diffuse technocratic and economic notions' (Georgi, 2010, 56) such as 'best practices' or 'improved standards of living', was also influenced by the numerous publications promoting the application of managerial logic to different aspects of life. Since the 1980s, this pervading managerial mindset, has led to individual subjectivation processes based on concepts such as employability, for which self-management is paramount (Boltanski, Chiapello, 2005). New public management is also tied to the growth of the migration industry and the involvement of private actors in migration reflects the advance of neoliberalism (Menz, 2013). In this drive for privatisation, employers or private agents through outsourcing are tasked with controlling compliance with migration status, determining workers' eligibility, etc. This does not necessarily mean that the state relinquishes its responsibilities over migration, but that another layer of management is added.

The International Organisation of Migration (IOM) brought the new public management approach to the political arena (Georgi, 2010). In the 2000s, an international migration regime was outlined by the New International Regime for Orderly Movements of People (NIROMP) project (GCIM, 2005; Ghosh, 2000), which considered migration could be coherently managed based primarily on economic criteria. Thus aiming to maximise benefits and reduce costs, while at the same time controlling migration flows from a 'neutral', bureaucratic, and depoliticised standpoint. This means conflicting or sensitive issues such as restricting workers to a single employer, or extending employers' supervisory role to make them responsible for enforcing migration policies, in an attempt to use fewer government resources, can be excluded or overlooked, as implemented measures are portrayed as technical.

Similarly, the Global Forum on Migration and Development launched in 2007 and the United Nations High-Level Dialogue on International Migration and Development fuelled renewed international interest in the topic (Bedford, R., et al., 2017). New Zealand and almost all OECD countries had established temporary migration programmes by the mid-2000s (OECD, 2008).[1] This new generation of circular migration schemes, implied a paradigmatic shift due to the assumption that the promotion of regulated options would deter the use of non-regulated channels, thus justifying migration management as a way of preventing irregular migration and security incidents. The inclusion of migration in the United Nations Sustainable Development Goals (SDGs) in 2015, and the launch of the Global Compact for Safe, Orderly and Regular Migration (GCM) in 2018,[2] consolidated and formalised the link between migration and development in international policy-making circles, with a variety of agents operating between and beyond national borders. Nonetheless, the link between

---

[1] See Dun et al. (2023) for a recent review of contemporary managed migration programmes with an agricultural focus/component.

[2] Pacific countries participating in the RSE scheme and New Zealand have adopted the GCM. However, only Fiji has signed the United Nations International Convention on the Protection of the Rights of All Migrant Workers and Members of their Families.

migration and development had already become increasingly visible since the 1990s, with remittances at the core of the 'development mantra' (Kapur, 2004). Around the same time, discussions of a 'global migration crisis' in international circles pointed to ineffective and incoherent policies having the potential to create crises (Weiner, 1995). Thus, norms and regulations were deemed essential to improve migration governance.

Under migration management, governments prioritise cost-effective migration policies and divert attention from migration issues that may be deemed controversial. Similarly, the uptake of new public management implied institutional and ideological changes in relation to cost shifting and blame avoidance (Menz, 2011, 2013), placing the financial burden and responsibility in cases of non-compliance or accidents on private actors, including employers and service providers. This pragmatic approach to migration blurs responsibilities between state and private actors. Presenting the management of migration as a technical problem requires the identification of policies and good or best practices to find 'what works'. This paradigmatic change led to the systematisation of mechanisms for managing migration which disavow migrant social relations and can curtail freedoms and rights in favour of demonstrating the effectiveness of migration programmes.

1.2 A Governmentality Framework and Neoliberalism

Governmentality is concerned with the ways of thinking and acting involved in governing for the benefit of populations' wealth, health, and happiness (Rose, Miller, 2010). Deciding what is considered beneficial for a population entails a political aspect beyond the apparent neutrality of the means of governing, prompting a process by which problems are made visible. Such a political process can be difficult to trace, given that problems appear in different places and times and for a variety of actors. Agents such as academic scholars, thematic experts, and government officials, can help decision-makers define problems, becoming part of an epistemic community. This problematisation suggests that problems are not waiting to be revealed, but instead need to be constructed (Miller, Rose, 2008) using specific forms of reasoning to understand reality, called rationalities.

The articulation of rationalities leads to an agreement about what the problems are. Problems are then framed using a common language – a narrative – which is distilled from policies and official discourses to quotidian interactions, allowing knowledge to be formalised, and enabling decision-makers to set measures to rectify said problems. From a state standpoint, governmentality techniques propose practicable interventions to remedy conducts that are deemed unproductive or inefficient. Thus, solutions to specific problematisations are put into practice by means of strategies, tactics and government programmes which range from 'governing the self' to 'governing others' (Lemke, 2007). These techniques are not concerned with legal subjects but with empirical quantities (Foucault, 2001), meaning not with citizens, but with populations. Population as data is the objective of governmental technologies and the political economy is the science and the technique for government intervention in the economy (Foucault, 1991). In this way, governing the conduct of the population couples economic and political imperatives through intervening in the complex relations populations have, not only with material resources, but also with different actors and their ways of thinking and acting.

Statistics are a classic example of a governmental technique, highly valued for policy-making because they facilitate decision-making. Statistics also reveal that 'through its movements, its customs, and its activity, population has specific economic effects' (Foucault, 2007). However, numbers and statistical data hide personal experiences, which are hard to quantify, and the subjects behind statistical figures can be instrumentalised to drive economic growth, becoming contingent on economic conditions. Under neoliberalism, the individual 'being himself his own capital, being for himself his own producer, being for himself the source of his earnings and entrepreneur of himself' (Foucault, 2008, 226), implies recognising individuals as labour units. This labour can then be broken down into income and skills, whereby personal skills determine where individuals would be able to work.

Foucauldian inspired studies on migration have mostly focused on the analysis of security and disciplining techniques. Security techniques are largely concerned with surveillance mechanisms and technological fixes, such as photographing, x-raying, and fingerprinting to meet visa requirements and border controls. In contrast, discipline allows the body to increase its economic productivity and at the same time weakens its forces 'to assure political subjection' (Lemke, 2011, 36). Discipline can encourage migration to become a waged worker, competition for productivity gains, or avoidance of health risks to remain productive. Discipline transforms the thinking, acting, and being of individuals through self-disciplining mechanisms and norms (Foucault, 1980), which can be considered prescriptions and truths, and as such can remain unquestioned. Discipline can also establish hierarchies and 'a division between those considered normal and abnormal, suitable and capable, and the others' (Lemke, 2011, 47), separating employable individuals from the unemployable.

While discipline may be associated with coercion, self-care is another technique more clearly associated to personal freedom and autonomous self-control capacities. With the exercise of self-care, individuals become subjects of their own actions. Self-care also enables social relations, as it allows a person to be in relation to others, whether that would be living in a community or having employment relations. For example, migrant workers, aware of behavioural rules at the workplace and the relations between self and others, regulate themselves to continue being part of their own workplace community. Self-care also problematises social risks – such as unemployment and lack of development – transferring responsibility to individuals and collectives, and relying on their moral rational choices to solve them (Lemke, 2001). Self-care is also one of the main tenets of a neoliberal rationality.

Understanding neoliberalism as a political rationality allows examining how its strategies are articulated. Neoliberalism renders the social domain as economic by emphasising personal responsibility or self-care. In doing so, neoliberalism does not necessarily opposes collectivism, but it rather promotes self-reliant communities (Rose, 2000). Persons are not governed as citizens but as member of communities by intensifying their allegiance to them under common objectives, in this case, 'enjoying development'. The driving principle for the neoliberal articulation of migration management is the maximisation of labour and money. Thus, in an epistemological break, neoliberalism shifts the object of economic analysis to the strategic programming of individuals' activity. This means not considering the worker as the object of supply and demand in the form of labour power, but as an active economic subject whose work is an 'economic conduct practiced, implemented, rationalized and calculated by the person who works' (Foucault, 2008, 223). In the upcoming sections, the linkages between governments' conduct of the economy to the conduct of individuals and their communities is brought to the foreground. Because practices are embedded in a particular rationality, identifying the kind of political knowledge underpinning them, becomes a valuable exercise.

1.3 Migration Management as the Governmentality of Mobility

Managing migration entails governing populations, regulating formal migration channels, defining policies, processes, and stakeholders and formalising their roles and responsibilities to avoid irregular migration. In contrast to other welfare forms, the neoliberal underpinnings of migration management aim to delegate public policy responsibilities to migrants to solve their own poverty or unemployment. Thus, migration management can be understood as the governmentality of mobility. Foucauldian scholars articulate migration management as a political rationality within neoliberal governmentality, as its effects are directed by employing discrete tools, disciplinary tactics and technologies (Kalm, 2010; Kunz, 2013). These range from 'information campaigns and "pre-departure instruments" (such as language training and tests, marriage and health checks, or measures putting an end to migration such as "voluntary assisted return" or resettlement activities)'

(Geiger, 2013, 31). These mechanisms of power have gained legitimacy through narratives, which uphold the roles of the managers of mobility and discipline migrant workers and their communities by instrumentalising development.

The conduct of migrants is regulated by particular governmental techniques that enact incentives for becoming a compliant migrant worker, and disincentives to become unproductive. Migrants, given the opportunity, are expected to behave as good rational actors, and their migratory experience is expected to catalyse other income generating activities. Linking migration with development narratives formalises the behavioural rules required to achieve development. Thus, the concern with analysing how political rationalities to enhance the welfare of migrants and the population more generally, are constructed through the power relations among different actors, such as academics, government officials, industry representatives, and policy advisers at national and international levels. Formalising a new visa-based channel to discourage unregulated migration and promote development can make regulated migration attractive for both policymakers and migrants. Conversely, the negative aspects or unintended consequences of managed migration, such as its implications for labour or civil rights, often remain unexplored by sending and receiving countries.

Arguments for development are conveyed at different stages of the migration process using a common idiom – development narratives – shared by policymakers, government officials, and workers. The processes and systems through which persons become migrants, known as the migration apparatus, perpetuate and emphasise this common narrative. Understanding mobility as an investment choice to improve household income, allows migration to be brought back to the economic analysis within the realm of human capital 'as behavior in terms [of] individual enterprise, of enterprise of oneself with investments and incomes' (Foucault, 2008, 230) and not as mechanisms that persons cannot control. Governmental techniques at different levels and stages of the migration process, transform social relations and cultural practices through a configuration of rationalities – knowledges – and conceptions of the subject (Marttila, 2013). Thus, a governmentality approach to temporary migration, allows us to examine the operation of different governmentality techniques, acknowledging the neoliberal rationalities involved, how they are deployed in relation to development, and how they transform social norms and ultimately migrants' subjectivities.

1.4 Temporary Migration Programmes and the 'Triple Win'

The long mainstream consensus between international organisations and governments regarding the economic development benefits of labour migration (Faist, Fauser & Kivisto, 2011), highlights the role of remittances in trickling down these benefits. Migration management programmes are often promoted as a 'triple win' solution given they are expected to benefit sending, receiving countries and migrants' communities. The monetary, material, and social remittances that migrants transfer to their communities are also considered a primary source for development, and migrants the primary agents of change (Faist, 2008; Kapur, 2004; Levitt, 1998; Naïr, 1997). Migration becomes no longer the prerogative of receiving states but can also involve sending countries and the migrants seeking to benefit from this type of labour mobility (Skeldon, 2010). This resonates with a 'third way' approach in which migrants are 'empowered' when given the primary responsibility for achieving development.

Development is thus portrayed as happening 'from below'. This approach aims for a positive view of migrants as 'partners in development' (Libercier, Schneider, 1996) and 'active or enterprising' citizens (Dean, 1999) given they are enabled by their governments to provide aid to their communities (Kapur, 2004), and so help themselves by managing their own needs. Migration management has also shifted concerns around development in migrants' communities of origin, to eventually replace external aid with the help of migrants' achievements. Migrants are conceived as entrepreneurs and are expected to use their gains – economic and soft skills – for productive purposes. This win-win-win scenario – and the narratives it entails – by which temporary migration provides employment and training opportunities for workers, bringing money into their households and local economy, and more widely economic growth and development, explicitly drives many of the current temporary migration programmes globally.

The 'triple win' narrative is built on the recognition that labour migration benefits destination countries because it eases labour needs, particularly in sectors that are deemed seasonal such as agriculture or tourism (GCIM, 2005; IOM, 2004). Development in migrants' countries of origin is expected to occur as the pressures created by unemployment are relieved, and through the arrival of remittances and knowledge transfer. This narrative also assumes similar interests of the parties involved and negates power differentials and conflicts (Geiger, Pécoud, 2010) among and within countries. This mainstream characterisation of migration management as apolitical and technocratic can be challenged as knowledge presented as factual, objective, and neutral is nevertheless informed by specific political assumptions and biases. Notions of neutrality and objectivity themselves always rest on epistemic and political assumptions. For example, migration can be a virtuous circle from a neoclassical or neoliberal economic standpoint, while a vicious one from a Marxist political economy, dependency theory, or a 'world systems' approach (King, 2018).

On the one hand, critics of the 'triple win' argument argue that destination countries are the winners as they receive 'labour without people', or circular migrants with ill-defined rights, making it easier for employers to exploit workers and engage in flexible hiring and firing, in line with economic and business conditions and short-term savings in integration costs (Wickramasekara, 2011). The economic inequalities within and among countries, which are the cornerstone of temporary migration, create a demand for cheap labour that can be mobilised between countries with wage differentials. On the other hand, proponents of the 'triple win' argue for the increase of competitiveness in destination countries by reducing costs and using flexible labour through migration management, instead of favouring more empowering welfare policies that could also promote development.

1.5 A Case Study from the Western Pacific

Since the RSE scheme was launched in 2007, the number of workers travelling to New Zealand was gradually increasing until COVID-19 disrupted seasonal mobility in early 2020. Up to 2022, over 36,600 Pacific citizens have participated in the scheme, the majority of them from Vanuatu (Bedford, R., Bedford, C., 2023). The appeal to analyse labour mobility of ni-Vanuatu goes beyond Vanuatu being the first country to pilot the RSE scheme in 2006. For decades, before the scheme's introduction, the country lacked labour migration except to New Caledonia, and its net migration was negligible (Hayes, 2010). In practice, mobility in Vanuatu was domestically limited to plantation workers, house girls, and other services and internationally as seafarers. This allowed discerning some transformations that the RSE scheme produced, particularly in communities where for most participants, this was their first formal employment. New contractual relations and financial commitments implied learning how to become contract waged workers and manage their own expenses to maximise remittances.

How learning is internalised and workers' associated understandings are nonetheless coloured by ni-Vanuatu customary worldviews, such as cultural practices of reciprocity (Smith, 2018, 2019), respect to authorities and elders, and a communal sense of belonging. These elements that can be considered as central for an anthropological study are also key for a governmentality analysis. Workers built on existing skills and post-colonial capitalist practices to engage in a transaction to sell their labour. The work ethic they adopt to 'succeed' conforms to a neoliberal entrepreneurial logic under which individuals produce their own advantages by delivering more than what their contract demands within and outside working hours, inside and outside work premises, and from recruitment to return. From my positionality as a non-ni-Vanuatu woman from the Global South, I acknowledge both cultural similarities and limitations of my own comprehension as the myriad of local differences in Vanuatu makes cultural generalisations impossible. Despite idiosyncrasies, new social relations are entangled in neoliberal values, which at times are at odds with more traditional customary ones and at others capitalise on them. Thus, the focus on how ni-Vanuatu interpret the new relations temporary migration produces.

This detailed research, builds on my doctoral dissertation (Astonitas, 2018). It is based on content analysis of documents, empirical experiences, and semi-structured interviews with ni-Vanuatu participants in the RSE scheme, policy-makers, labour inspectors, pastoral care workers, tutors, and community members between 2014 and 2015. It encompassed two different agricultural seasons in Hawke's Bay, New Zealand (see Figure 1) and an in-between period when participants had returned to their villages nearby Port Vila and Santo, the main urban centres in Vanuatu (see Figure 2). This phased-design involved interviews with the same workers across their migration journey at different points in time and in different locations, visiting their communities and transit places as can be seen in Table 1. To protect participants at the core of this research, pseudonyms are used.

Important transformations brought about by the coupling of migration and development could already be discerned then and are relevant for current political discussions about agricultural temporary workers' welfare in the

Table 1 Fieldwork details

	New Zealand	Vanuatu	New Zealand
Timeframe	2013–2014 Agricultural season	October – November 2014	2014–2015 Agricultural season
Location	• Hawke's Bay	• Efate • Santo	• Hawke's Bay • Nelson
Participants	• 25 RSE workers	• 21 RSE workers • 6 family, community, and village members • 2 Vanuatu Department of Labour representatives	• 23 RSE workers • 9 labour inspectors, government officers, industry leaders, pastoral care workers, and workers' tutors

Development Subjectivities and Governmentality 13

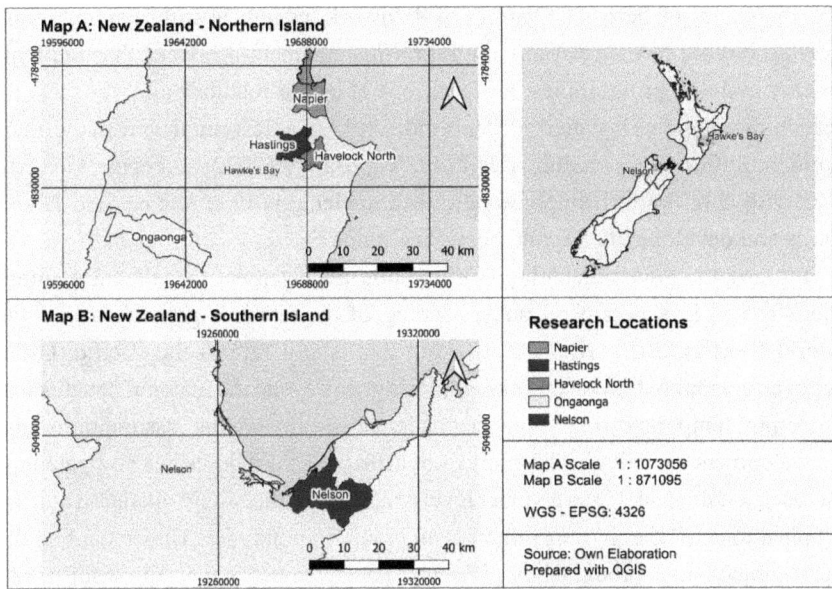

Figure 1 New Zealand research locations

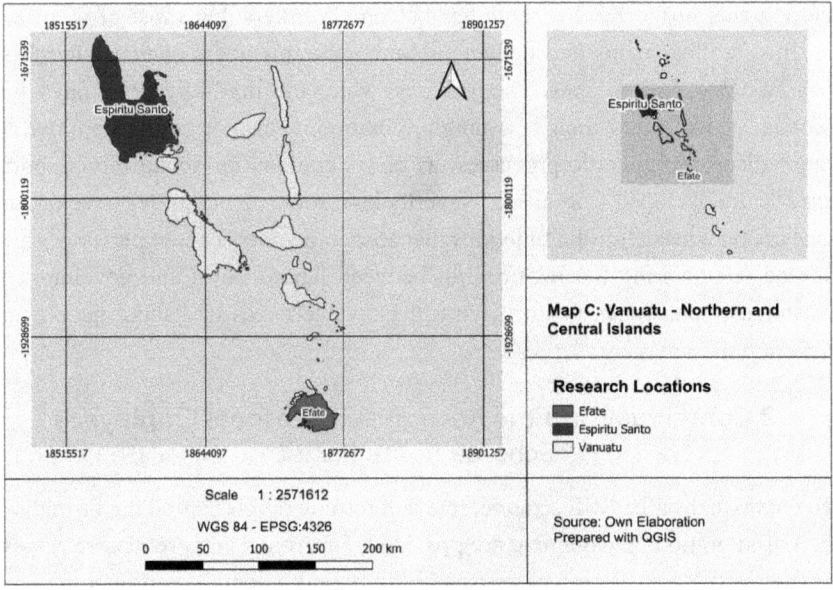

Figure 2 Vanuatu research locations

Pacific and elsewhere. The variety of fieldwork insights is still pertinent today and applicable to the relations migration management produces through temporary mobility programmes. A closer look at labour relations after the COVID pandemic, which classified agricultural workers as essential and made their vulnerabilities more visible (Bedford, C., Bailey, 2022; Liangni, Guanyu, Xiaoyun, 2022) attach importance to acknowledging migrants beyond labour units and development beyond economic gains.

Linking the governmentality of migration management to political assumptions rooted in a neoliberal understanding of migration is growing across the world (Bartels, 2017; Karal, 2018), but this is still rare in the Pacific. Using a governmentality framework, this analysis goes beyond the material benefits that underpin temporary migration to challenge its underlying assumptions and 'development narrative'. The analysis at different scales describes how relations at local, national, and international levels manifest in their daily operation and the implications for the lives of migrants and their communities. Understanding the new subjectivities produced by ni-Vanuatu engagement in their quest for development using a governmentality framework allows us to disentangle political and economic relations across borders.

By analysing the mundane day-to-day practices of governments and other actors inside and outside institutions, as well as policy prescriptions, a more nuanced understanding of the benefits and costs of migration surfaces. Participants in the RSE scheme are not only workers, but most of them are parents, siblings, sons and daughters, and active members of their churches, communities, and villages. Their bodies, which are tired after long days and months of work and their less tangible emotions, cannot be incorporated to rationalised technocratic processes, as considerations for social reproduction aspects are excluded from them. Nevertheless, some communities have organised to compensate for the functions that absent members cannot perform while abroad. Uncovering the relationship between labour flows and development narratives, contributes to identifying the diverse needs of Pacific peoples to inform policy-making.

2 Contextualising the Recognised Seasonal Employer's Scheme in the Pacific

To contextualise the RSE scheme, relevant turning points behind the formalisation of migration management are provided. Far from a comprehensive review of the evolving migration processes in the region, attention is drawn to some historical events shaping labour mobility in the Pacific. Since pre-contact times mobility in the Pacific has mostly been circular with intentions of returning to the original place of residence. Mobility facilitated social transformation and labour engagements and traditionally it was mostly men who moved. Nowadays, the RSE scheme and its equivalent in Australia, the Seasonal Worker Programme (SWP)[3] are also enmeshed in contemporary social transformation processes. An overview of the historical context framing how the scheme was designed, including how Pacific governments valued accessing labour markets in the region's most developed economies, provides a frame of reference. After the brief historical background on Pacific mobility and migration, follows an overview of labour mobility preceding the RSE scheme in New Zealand and the variety of roles stakeholders undertook in the design and operationalisation of the scheme.

2.1 Pacific Mobility and Labour Migration over Time

It is widely accepted that contemporary mobility in the Pacific is not a new phenomenon. The circular nature of mobility in the Pacific is understood as a continuation of long-standing mobility patterns (Bedford, R., Hugo, 2008) within customary lifestyles and with the purpose of expanding horizons and livelihood options. Pacific mobility from the 1930s onwards has been characterised as internal and circular, because the intention was often to return home. Circular migration studies in the 1970s and 1980s (Bedford, R., 1973; Chapman, 1986) considered these arrangements to be 'deeply rooted in a great variety of cultures and found at all stages of socio-economic exchange' (Chapman, Prothero, 1986, 6). Reasons for this mobility included changing ecological regimes, customary lifestyles, beliefs, values, and attitudes or decisions from the elderly or prestigious village members. Mobility facilitated social transformation and provided new opportunities for work. Similarly, later rural-urban migration responded to motivations ranging from searching for labour opportunities in capital cities or abroad, to visiting relatives, or pursuing further education. In the Western Pacific, men would travel routinely for several months leaving women with increased responsibilities (Jolly, 1987). Consciously motivated movement is highly valued (Hess, 2009) compared to wandering or enforced movement.

In the first half of the Nineteenth century, and until the Second World War, labour migration from the Pacific reached its peak. In the mid-Nineteenth century, the labour trade to Australia, Fiji, and New Caledonia mobilised over 60,000 Pacific Islanders, particularly from Vanuatu and the Solomon Islands (Munro, 1995). The 'blackbirds', as they were called, were many of them coerced, or lured by promises of great wealth. They worked mainly on sugar

---

[3] See Petrou and Connell (2023a) for a comprehensive analysis of the SWP, since 2022 part of the Pacific Australia Labour Mobility scheme.

plantations in Queensland needing labour intensive agriculture, and mining for rare commodities in New Caledonia towards the end of the century. Later, some resorted to other work such as fishing or on plantations (Moore, Leckie & Munro, 1990) becoming instrumental for conversion to Christianity when returning to their communities (Jolly, 2012). While labour became commodified, neither Vanuatu nor Solomon Islands had any formal migration outlets before the RSE scheme (Bedford, Hugo, 2008; Ramasamy et al., 2008) in contrast to other Pacific countries such as Samoa, Tonga, or Fiji. As would be later explained, some migration agreements between New Zealand and selected Pacific countries provided foreign labour to New Zealand industries, while in Vanuatu and Solomon Islands people continued moving within their country as they had done for generations, seafarers being a scant exception.

In the twentieth century, other forms of labour mobility from Pacific countries were established based on skilled work categories. For example, in Kiribati and Tuvalu, the recruitment of seafarers for international merchant vessels remained informal and thus unregulated or uncoordinated by national authorities until the mid-1960s. Under British colonial rule, a recruitment agency was established in 1969 to facilitate the international employment of young I-Kiribati and Tuvaluan men. After Tuvalu's and Kiribati's independence in 1978 and 1979 respectively, options for the employment of men seafarers, gradually extended from tuna companies to cruise liners and merchant vessels (Borovnik, 2009).[4] Women started being recruited for cruise ships' catering services in 2003 (Kagan, 2016). To date, men continue to outnumber women engaging in formal migration programmes by a substantial number.

In parallel, migration of highly skilled workers to Australia and New Zealand has steadily increased in the last decades, raising concerns about brain drain and becoming a bottleneck for development due to the fragility of Pacific countries' public education and health services. Development implications of high-skilled migration can be far-reaching, given the policy incentives to attract workers in areas of shortage in the two countries (Iredale, Voigt-Graf & Khoo, 2012; Yamamoto et al., 2012). The pressure of ageing populations in the region is also driving more permanent migration forms for care workers for both the young and elderly, a highly gendered sector (Badkar, Callister & Didham, 2009; Connell, Walton-Roberts, 2016; Hugo, 2009; Yamamoto et al., 2012). These jobs are associated to what is traditionally considered as women's care work, and are low paid, attracting fewer locals. Other more recent tradesmen temporary migrant worker programmes aimed at Pacific Islanders with post-school

---

[4] Borovnik (2011) describes the experiences of seafarers using a transnational conceptualisation of circular mobility (Borovnik, 2009) and showing a shift in Pacific identities (Borovnik, 2005) based on the complexities of how migrants connect to their families and places.

qualifications are capped at less than 2,000 workers per year (Curtain et al., 2018). The RSE scheme is designed in this context of co-existing labour migration programmes reliant on the skills of its participants and a relatively long history of Pacific labour migration.

2.2 Precursors to the RSE Scheme in New Zealand

The RSE scheme should be understood in the context of other temporary labour programmes that select migrants based on their specific attributes, which make them attractive for a country with labour shortages. Until 1987, New Zealand encouraged permanent settlers from certain countries of origin, but shifted its focus with the passing of a new Immigration Act (1987 No 74) so migrants with specific characteristics could be recruited (Wilson, P., Fry, 2020). This shift responds to the introduction of neoliberal reforms in the 1980s and 1990s, and government adoption of new public management approaches. Then, a managerial style was introduced to policy-making and governance, bringing in technical expertise and oversight to reduce the inefficiencies of public administration. This allowed the private sector to have a stronger role in the economy, not only as expert consultants, but also through outsourcing, delivering goods and services previously provided by the government.

The preferential status given to Pacific workers in the RSE scheme is historically based on temporary labour schemes in place since the 1960s (Bedford, C., 2013; Lovelock, Leopold, 2008). Pacific workers have engaged in the New Zealand labour market at different periods to address labour needs and because some countries had freedom of entry as part of decolonisation processes. In 1964, the 'Samoan Quota' began granting a certain number of Samoan visitors' permits to work. By 1967, the Temporary Employment Certificate aimed to regulate the flow of Fijians seeking employment but was suspended in 1969 because of increasing unemployment and an economic downturn in New Zealand (Māhina-Tuai, 2012). The Fiji Rural Work Permit Scheme was the first work permit introduced to regulate migration to New Zealand. It allowed Fijians to work in agriculture and later in halal slaughtering. Similarly to the RSE scheme, employers were required to provide 'satisfactory' accommodation for workers. Later, during the 1970s, these temporary schemes granted visas to work in the then booming manufacturing sector.

The South Pacific Work Permit Scheme (SPWPS) was created in 1977 to regulate the flow of Fijians, Samoans, and Tongans and was later extended to Tuvaluans and I-Kiribati. These government initiatives, as well as the Pacific Islands Industrial Development Scheme, were intended to regulate and formalise the movement of workers and illustrate a relationship between temporary migration and development initiatives in the region (Lovelock, Leopold, 2008). The SPWPS programme's arrangements with Fiji ended in 1987 following the coup d'état, and with Tonga and Samoa in 1991. By 2001, the programme had been terminated mainly due to Tuvaluans and I-Kiribati overstaying (Bedford, C., Bedford & Ho, 2010). Hayes (2010) considers the SPWPS as a precursor of the RSE scheme, because the responsibilities of employers and of the sending and receiving governments were specified in formal agreements. Nowadays, the RSE scheme coexists with other New Zealand government migration schemes that promote migration from Pacific Island countries on a regular basis,[5] some based on a ballot system and others granting residence pathways.

This brief recount of the New Zealand's migration schemes situates the RSE scheme in the wider historical context of labour mobility policies in the Pacific region. Besides the common characteristics shared with previous and current labour migration schemes, the management of the RSE scheme entails a policy shift towards regulating migration by establishing bilateral labour agreements between governments, which are a governmental technique in themselves. Such agreements do not establish legal relationships between the parties, but document negotiations on practical matters, defining policies, principles, roles, and relationships, thus becoming a necessary instrument for managing labour migration (Luthria, Malaulau, 2013). The social relations migrants create are not autonomous, but mediated by the material conditions enabled by different actors,[6] and how positively or negatively migration is portrayed at different points in time. Thus, the importance of understanding historical, geographical, and political conditions as well as the stakeholders involved in creating and upholding migration programmes. Besides policy-makers, industry associations in the horticulture and viticulture sectors were instrumental in driving the launch of the RSE scheme and have a fundamental role in its management.

2.3 The Demands of New Zealand Industry Associations

One of the differences between the variety of temporary migration schemes negotiated with different countries over time and the RSE scheme is the intervention of the private sector. New Zealand's horticulture and viticulture sectors mobilised their government, lobbying for the scheme's inception well before it was officially launched in 2007 (OECD, 2014) and were active in the pilot leading to its implementation. At that time, there were industry complaints about significant losses in their output and value added because of labour

---

[5] See Bedford et al. (2017), Friesen (2018), and Voigt-Graf and Kanemasu (2019) for further details on current programmes.

[6] See Collins (2020) for a stratification analysis according to migration status and associated rights, which locates RSE workers at the bottom of current migration channels to New Zealand.

shortages, which representatives claimed, was reducing these industries' ability for further investments. Complaints about the industry exploiting labour of unauthorised migrants through gang masters or contractors were commonplace. While the RSE scheme was industry-driven, specifically by the agriculture and viticulture commercial fruit and vegetable growers' associations, it entailed negotiations with the government to curtail illegal employment in the sector.

The scheme's initial uptake was encouraged by the labour force shortages that the industry experienced since the late 1990s, the high visibility of illegal workforce scams in the sector, and a low unemployment rate for New Zealanders. At that time, trafficking of foreign workers in the horticulture sector was an open secret that gained media attention. Migrants were illegally working and often exposed to abuses such as payment below the minimum wage, extensive shifts, or substandard accommodations in the largest growing areas (Coppedge, 2006; Courtney, 2008; Lovelock, Leopold, 2008; Sharpe, 2010). Working under precarious conditions, obviously creates pressure for workers to perform to their employer's satisfaction to prevent dismissal and potentially deportation, accepting poor working conditions, low wages and hard physical labour. This 'deportability' (De Genova, Peutz, 2010) is based on restrictions workers face, such as their use of time or limited participation in their host communities, and produces social relations marked by fear due to laws and discipline and the hierarchical relations with their employers.

The horticulture and viticulture sectors generally see the scheme in a positive light as it matches temporary workers with low paying work opportunities in their home countries, with industry seasonal labour needs. Likewise, Pacific governments had long advocated for labour mobility and access to labour markets in New Zealand and Australia, because they could not absorb their growing labour force (Bedford, Hugo, 2008). The New Zealand government acknowledged the RSE scheme could meet seasonal labour requirements at the most intensive time in the agricultural cycle and endorsed it as a solution to achieve sustainable economic growth, ensuring these industries could remain competitive in international markets. Employers acknowledge the RSE scheme's contribution to their firms' growth and productivity (Nunns, Bedford, C. & Bedford, R. 2019). Because international quality standards can be fulfilled when fruit is harvested at its optimal maturity, further investments are possible, such as the diversification of pipfruit varieties, and the expansion of cultivated areas (Bedford, C., Bedford, R. & Nunns, 2020; Ministry for Primary Industries, 2017; Plant & Food Research, 2016). Generally, the horticulture and viticulture industries have rapidly grown since the mid-2000s, as the demand for products in export markets has increased.

RSE scheme employers represent a small share of the horticulture and viticulture operations compared to the total number of agricultural employers in the country. The size of orchards and farms recruiting Pacific workers range from family businesses to large-scale agro-industrial export companies. The horticultural sector remains labour intensive despite its industrialisation. Over 80 per cent of jobs in the horticulture sector are short-term and related to time-bound tasks due to the seasonality of crops. Seasonal agricultural work is inherently insecure. It often requires moving outside urban areas, being compensated at the wages offered within the industry (Carens, 2008), which are ultimately driven by competition among agricultural export prices from other countries. Thus, in industrialised countries, this type of work can be unattractive for locals, or carried out under working conditions that do not meet domestic workers' expectations (Basok, 2002). It is not necessarily that there are no workers available, but not enough are willing to engage under the conditions temporary work entails. Some RSE workers have become 'permanently temporary' (Rajkumar et al., 2012), as workers return year after year,[7] to supply with work that not enough people are willing to do.

During 2008–2017, over 67,000 visas were granted to Pacific workers engaged in the RSE scheme, considerably less than the 93,000 visas granted to non-RSE scheme Pacific workers (Friesen, 2018). Nonetheless, since 2012 the number of RSE scheme visas has surpassed that of other types of temporary work visas approved for Pacific countries' citizens. These workers are a fraction of the international seasonal work migrants, such as tourists on working holiday visas[8] and temporary contractors the industry relies on during the harvest seasons. The scheme has grown and RSE workers make almost 20 per cent of peak employment (Petrou, Connell, 2023a). Industry associations continue lobbying for subsequent increases in seasonal caps, from 5,000 workers in 2007 to 19,500 in 2023.

2.4 Policy-makers and the RSE Scheme as a Development Instrument

The architects of the RSE scheme, not only responded to New Zealand industries, but also to the calls from Pacific Island Forum (PIF) countries for increased labour opportunities in New Zealand, to spur development in the Pacific Islands (Bedford, Hugo, 2008; PCF, 2013). The PIF is the premier political and economic policy organisation in the region. Besides aiming to

---

[7] In the first decade of the RSE scheme, workers' return rate was around 60 percent.
[8] See Opara (2018) for an analysis of temporary labour migration to New Zealand and wider societal impacts of the Working Holiday scheme.

foster intergovernmental cooperation and collaboration with international agencies, representing the interests of its member countries, the PIF has played a key role in economic restructuring, channelling the diffusion of neoliberal approaches among Pacific Island leaders in the last decades (Slatter, 2006). Recurrently conveyed at several annual conferences of South Pacific Labour Ministers, during the 1970s and early 1980s, their proposals for access to the largest economies labour markets remained unattended for years.

The process of economic development in the Pacific needs to consider past processes of change and how responses to regional or national change vary depending on the differential access to development opportunities (Connell, Lee, 2018). In many parts of the Pacific, capitalism was not much a means of economic development, but strategies that favoured privatisation and more effective governance, whose lexicons were absorbed into indigenous practices (Connell, 2010) as citizens were encouraged to incorporate notions of progress and eschew tradition. Pacific scholars criticise the adoption of Western political and economic systems because they encourage dependency and privilege economic interests (Hau'ofa, 1994; Kabutaulaka, 2015). Portraying development as Westernisation is also problematic, as local ways of knowing, doing, and being still have a crucial role in Pacific worldviews. Alongside this comprehension of Pacific peoples' needs, top down notions of aid from developed countries have strongly influenced development policies in the region.

In the preparatory discussions prior to the implementation of the RSE scheme, policy-makers from New Zealand and Pacific countries gathered in a government sponsored forum (Plimmer, 2006). Discussions focused on overseas employment as a solution to unstable and weak governance, public sector inefficiencies, and the high aid dependency of Pacific countries. In alignment with a neoliberal policy approach of entrepreneurship and self-care and the downsizing of international aid, widening the reach of labour opportunities was seen as a solution for public sector deficits that could no longer support the same level of aid provided to Pacific countries in previous decades. Within this rationale, the employment of Pacific Island citizens in the RSE scheme, was considered essential for local development and economic growth. Since then, New Zealand and Pacific government officials and politicians alike have frequently portrayed remittances and other economic gains from the scheme as development aid provided to Pacific countries. Capitalising on remittances had been already high in their agenda and calls for measures to increase remittance flows are still commonplace (MBIE, 2015; MFAT, 2018; PIFS, 2005b).

In terms of international economic relations, access to Australian and New Zealand labour markets by unskilled workers, has historically been a central interest for PIF Countries in regional trade talks under PICTA (Pacific Island

Countries Trade Agreement), PACER (Pacific Agreement on Closer Economic Relations), and PACER Plus (Hugo, Bedford, 2017; Maclellan, Mares, 2006). The PICTA, signed in 2001, was expanded to cover trade in services, including temporary mobility (Voigt-Graf, Kanemasu, 2019). Commitments on labour mobility and development assistance were important inclusion points for Pacific countries during the lengthy negotiations towards the signature of PACER Plus. Both issues were contentious and excluded from the agreement as Australia and New Zealand would arguably be forced to extend similar commitments to other free trade agreements signed with non-Pacific countries. Labour mobility of low-skilled workers, which is the classification that RSE workers receive, is currently addressed in a non-legally binding side agreement called the 'Arrangement on Labour Mobility', not part of PACER Plus but monitored alongside it.

More recently, the introduction of the Pacific Reset initiative from the New Zealand government in 2018, aims to reaffirm its role as both a regional leader and a partner and re-engage its Pacific Island neighbours. This strategy is a reaction to increased interest and competition in the region, predominantly from China, and privileges the provision of aid to Pacific Island countries by appealing to a common identity. Drawing on the commonality of interests and the notion of New Zealand as a Pacific country, the government aims to broaden its relative regional influence in terms of national security and shared prosperity. This responds to a shift towards 'new public diplomacy', whereby a two-way country engagement is privileged (Mark, 2022). A key principle of this strategy is to strive for mutually benefitting solutions when developing domestic and foreign policy, such as with the RSE scheme, which entails beneficial policy objectives for Pacific countries and New Zealand (Bedford, C., Bedford, R. & Nunns, 2020). Similarly, some Pacific countries have included labour migration as a key element in their national policies. The COVID outbreak, its travel restrictions, the human rights review of the RSE scheme (NZHRC, 2022) and the latest cyclone seasons brought increased attention to the scheme, while strong sectoral lobbying continuously supports the inward flow of workers.

2.5 The Operationalisation of the RSE Scheme

In 2006, the World Bank supported a pilot programme involving 45 ni-Vanuatu workers, which entered New Zealand under an already available visa to recruit foreign workers through the Approval in Principle process. This pilot encouraged and consolidated the ties 'that led to Vanuatu ultimately being the largest participant in the scheme' (McKenzie, Gibson, 2014, 5). Nonetheless, this preference has also been attributed to employers' interest in reducing possibilities for absconding, given the lack of a local ni-Vanuatu diaspora (Petrou, Connell, 2023a; Voigt-Graf, Kanemasu, 2019). Employers who proved their labour needs could not be met locally, could sponsor foreign workers, conditional to meeting immigration requirements. After the success of the pilot, five Pacific countries were selected to kick-start the scheme in 2007: Vanuatu, Samoa, Tonga, Kiribati, and Tuvalu. Of these five Pacific countries, only Vanuatu lacked an institutionalised migration programme. Later, the scheme was extended to nationals from other countries in the Pacific region, such as Solomon Islands (2010) and Fiji (2014). Papua New Guinea nationals were working in the RSE scheme without a bilateral agreement until 2013, when an Interagency Understanding with New Zealand was signed.

The management of the RSE scheme is based on formal bilateral agreements between governments outlining the conditions for its operation (Luthria, Malaulau, 2013). For example, defining the content of mandatory pre-departure trainings for all participant workers and workers' team leaders, which comprise from payslip explanations to behavioural recommendations. The scheme's main operational aspects/principles have not substantially changed since its inception (IMSED Research, 2010; INZ, 2010), these cover:

- Employer recognition – Employers apply for RSE status, which entails qualifying as a good employer, demonstrating financial viability, high standard human resource policies and workplace practices, capacity to provide 'suitable' accommodation for workers, and compliance with employment laws. Once employers achieve RSE status, they apply for an Agreement to Recruit (ATR) specifying the number of overseas workers needed, location, timeframe, and tasks.
- New Zealanders first – Employers have to demonstrate sensible efforts to recruit New Zealanders before recruiting resident or foreign workers. This is often done in connection with Work & Income New Zealand, the government agency that supports employers to fill in vacancies. The number of workers approved in ATRs is subject to the availability of national workers.
- Pacific preference – Employers are only allowed to recruit non-Pacific workers if their employment relation predates the RSE scheme inception.
- Employer driven – The employers select who to employ as well as who to re-employ in successive seasons, at their own discretion. Employers usually base this selection on workers' behaviour and productivity. Prospective employers can recruit workers directly or via paid labour agents. In Vanuatu employers arrange network recruiting and there are only few agents.
- Short-term migration – Workers are granted a limited purpose visa for the timeframe established in their employer's ATR; for a maximum of seven

months during an eleven-month period in an agricultural season. Citizens from Kiribati and Tuvalu are exceptionally allowed to stay up to nine months because of their higher travel costs. These limited visas tie a worker to an employer. Workers are not able to change employers while in New Zealand and employers are responsible for overseeing workers' return to their home countries. A joint ATR involving more than one employer allows participants to work for different employers, sometimes in a different town or island.[9]

- Circular migration – The return of workers benefits employers from productivity gains derived from previous seasons training and experience. Additionally, to be able to travel/return to New Zealand workers should have an offer of employment and meet immigration requirements, such as good character, health, and acceptance criteria for medical insurance to be granted a visa.
- Pastoral care – The employer is responsible for guidance and support of workers, which could be done in house or hiring a third party. Pastoral care workers often coordinate transportation (to and from ports of arrival/departure as well as worksites), supervise suitable accommodation and onsite facilities, and facilitate access to personal banking and personal protective equipment. Besides logistical support, they deal with grievances and may provide language translation when needed.

The RSE scheme's emphasis on economic development encouraged complementary training programmes for stakeholders under two initiatives: Toso Vaka o Manū, formerly Strengthening Pacific Partnerships, and the Vakameasina, Learning for Pacific Growth programme. The first is funded by New Zealand's Ministry of Foreign Affairs and Trade (MFAT) through the New Zealand Aid Programme (NZAid), and supports Pacific states to strengthen management capacities within the RSE scheme in the areas of information management, knowledge, processes, communications, and marketing for migrant workers. While the Toso Vaka o Manū is heavily inclined towards government officials, the Vakameasina is intended for workers, to 'enhance development gains' from the RSE scheme (OECD, 2011). The Vakameasina is managed by a consulting company which delivers English and financial literacy, and numeracy trainings besides topics selected by workers. Participants attend these sessions after their regular working hours (Taylor, Scarrow, 2010). Participation depends on employers' requests for training, facilitators and workers availability. Shift work, long summertime working days, harvesting and packing periods, also limit workers' opportunities for off-work related daily chores such as grocery shopping, cooking, and leisure time, which can become a barrier for attendance.

---

[9] Under COVID, joint ATRs facilitated moving to different companies in other locations (Bedford, Bailey, 2022).

During its first decade, the scheme operated without substantial modifications to how it was designed and its value was mostly assessed in terms of its contribution to New Zealand's primary sectors (Nunns, Bedford, C. & Bedford, R., 2019). While published research (Gibson, Bailey, 2021; McKenzie, Gibson, 2014) and grey literature focused on productivity, workforce reliability and investment expansion, assessments of the social outcomes of the scheme are recently gaining more attention (Bailey, Bedford, 2020; Bedford, Bailey, 2022; NZHRC, 2022), particularly due to the implications of COVID restrictions and the increasing number of participants engaging in the restart of the formerly Australian SWP in 2020 and its overall effects on Pacific labour markets.

2.6 Pacific Workers in New Zealand

Though employment opportunities for unskilled workers are arguably gender-neutral, employers favour men. Women mostly deal with specialised tasks such as grafting fruit onto rootstock, picking up berries, grounding cover crops, or working inside the packing house (Astonitas, 2018; Bedford, C., Bedford, R. & Nunns, 2020); thus they have fewer opportunities for work. Roughly, a thousand women participated in the scheme from 2015 to 2020, but their participation share dropped from 13.5% in 2014/2015 to 9.8% in 2018/2019 (Bedford, C., Bedford, R. & Nunns, 2020). Conversely, non-RSE scheme visas provide more opportunities for women. More non-RSE scheme visas have been granted to women from Fiji (44%), Tonga (36%), and Samoa (31%) over the last 20 years (Friesen, 2018). Non-Pacific workers in the RSE scheme represent less than 20 per cent of the total number of participants to date. Overall, RSE workers represent less than 0.5% of New Zealand total employment (Gibson, Bailey, 2021).

RSE scheme workers are mostly visible when they are working. This is because workers are housed together, but often separately from local communities. In some regions such as Central Otago, the increasing number of seasonal migrants has changed the landscape of the vineyards (Bailey, 2014) and small towns. In other areas, lodging migrant workers inside the premises of the companies they work for and having sporadic or no contact with the local communities, especially if they live in isolated rural areas, results in a 'sanitised landscape' (Overton, Murray, 2013) whereby workers' imprint is minimised in the countryside, as their households remain in workers' countries of origin where their social reproduction occurs. Other factors that restrict workers' possibilities of engaging with local communities are the lack of public transportation in rural areas or their lack of access to a means of transport. Living where they work and at the same time, working where they live also blurs the lines between their working and non-working hours.

Although labour mobility under the RSE scheme appears to be small in terms of numbers, it is important to consider the distribution of participants as a percentage of the sending countries' population, particularly when people selected belong to the same village, as it is often the case. In Vanuatu, slightly over 5 per cent of the population has participated in the scheme, over half of them in 2 or more seasons (Bedford, R., Bedford, C., 2023). This has implications for essential social reproduction aspects pertaining to daily duties of village lives and the burdens faced by local communities in workers' home countries which may experience the negative consequences of families being separated (Bailey, Bumseng & Bumseng, 2016; Clear Horizon, 2016).[10] Until recently, not much attention had been given to the reasons behind the inequitable access to this type of mobility for some Pacific people (Bedford, C. Bedford, R. & Nunns, 2020; Underhill-Sem et al., 2019). Far from levelling the play field, the preferential treatment for a few countries facilitated measures that increased the participation of the 'Big 3' – Vanuatu, Samoa, and Tonga, currently filling almost 85 per cent of all available jobs. Under these circumstances, democratising access to these opportunities among different regions in all the participating Pacific countries remains a challenge.

COVID places additional economic and personal challenges for Pacific workers. New Zealand's and Pacific countries strict border closures meant that a large number of workers were not able to return to their home countries, some staying for over six months up to almost three years beyond their original contract.[11] Similarly, it became difficult for new workers to enter New Zealand, despite most Pacific Island countries remained largely COVID free until 2021. Pacific countries also resisted their citizens being recruited to prevent COVID arrivals. This threatened the sustainability of the RSE scheme and surfaced the working conditions that workers face in everyday agroindustry operations (Bedford, Bailey, 2022; Collins, 2021; Petrou, Connell, 2023b). With no earning from fruit picking, the New Zealand government implemented a financial support package (Bedford, C. & Bailey, R., 2022) as it was difficult for workers to pay for regular expenses such as food and accommodation. They were also less able to communicate and send money to their families that were awaiting their return. Though my fieldwork covered from 2014 to 2016, workers' well-being and vulnerabilities described in section 4 became more evident under COVID restrictions and more recently due to the increase of Pacific workers travelling to Australia after borders reopened.

---

[10] To better support workers and families respond to marital challenges and children issues Vanuatu aims to develop a Community of Care model in 2024.

[11] Before March 2020 about 3,500 RSE and 4,500 SWP workers were caught in New Zealand and Australia respectively (Bailey, Bedford, 2020).

3 Governmentality in the RSE Scheme

New Zealand can be considered a migration state (Adamson, Tsourapas, 2020) due to its high reliance on migration. From international tourists, to university students, not only Pacific migrants are regularly incorporated into the labour force within a variety of temporary visa streams. In the early 2000s, New Zealand policies shifted towards the regulation of temporary visas that restrict or delay access to citizenship paths (Collins, 2020; Liangni, Guanyu, Xiaoyun, 2022). Nonetheless, the entanglement of both developmental and neoliberal state typologies (Adamson, Tsourapas, 2020) are evidenced in the management of the RSE scheme. Grounded on long-standing historical relations between the diverse countries in the Pacific and New Zealand, different governmental techniques, advance neoliberal rationalities to encourage 'development' through the operationalisation and the mundane ways in which the scheme is implemented. The problematisation of poverty, unemployment, and population growth, as well as the means used to solve these problems reflect neoliberal rationalities and Western values. Their extrapolation to recently formed states which are not fully capitalistic and rely on semi-subsistence economies, transform local ways of knowing and doing intertwining them with Western worldviews.

Migration management in the RSE scheme is demand-driven and entails international cooperation because of the multiple roles of a diversity of actors involved across borders. For example, market needs in New Zealand's horticultural and viticultural sectors circumscribe and restrict allowed activities for employers and workers under the scheme. Thus, the harmonisation of policies and negotiation of interests of participating countries, international agreements, and the linkages with other stakeholders having a role in policy-making such as international organisations, private sector representatives, and technical experts becomes crucial. The asymmetry of institutional and political conditions among different countries, places less developed economies in a disadvantageous position to incorporate policies devised in more developed ones. Drawing on the narratives of epistemic communities evidenced through the content analysis of policy documents, and expert interviews with government officers and industry leaders from both New Zealand and Vanuatu, the underlying power relations informing policy discourses, practices, narratives, and processes of subjectivation are brought to the surface.

The technocratic migration management model underpinning the RSE scheme is paired with an extensive operation involving a network of stakeholders in both sending and receiving countries, including the migrant workers and their communities (Bedford, C., Bedford R. & Nunns, 2020). For the RSE scheme to work, each segment of the population governed requires a functioning system reliant on the behaviour and relationships of the different public and private actors involved. The rationale of attending to the welfare of Pacific populations, through the solutions 'development' could bring, plays out in the migration management proposal to orderly manage semi-skilled labour mobility. This analysis does not argue against or for the regulation of migration, but surfaces the relations produced thereby.

3.1 The Problematisation of Unemployment and the Pacific Youth Bulge

The problematisation of being simultaneously unemployed and young in the region responds to concerns closely related to security in the Southern Pacific. The definition of unemployment, understood as the number of people looking for work, differs from country to country, sometimes not being a reliable measure. In the Pacific region, calculations of formal and informal employment and the lack of up-to-date data and changes in methodologies in census data categories (Connell, 1984) can also mask unemployment real dimensions. This hasty application of the concept of unemployment to semi-subsistence economies in countries that are not fully capitalistic is debatable at the very least, given that subsistence activities are not accounted as part of domestic economic performance indicators. The non-monetarily quantified economic activities entailing social reproduction aspects of local communities, as well as the skills required to participate in a subsistence economy are not considered into estimations of productivity either.

Similarly, the classification of different abilities typecast the skilled and the unskilled. On the one hand, are the highly qualified professionals who based on their relationship to the businesses they work for, can create monetary value (Truong, 2011). On the other, are the unskilled who are less valued by their economic activities per se, or by the amount of labour they contribute to their subsistence. Agricultural workers develop experience-based skills to understand the cycles of nature, optimal times for planting and harvesting, among other valuable skills required in subsistence economies, which are not remunerated or accounted for at the same level as any other work requiring proficiency, due to the assumption that these activities require no training. The construction of the unemployed category according to different definitions influences how policies are enacted and how individuals and specific groups understand themselves in relation to others. Thus, unemployment figures at the higher end could reflect the untapped potential of a population segment that could become productive if the right policies were in place. This argument favours mobilising labour from places where it is not remunerated to places where it is.

The security argument has a long history as a political strategy for imposing policies in the region. Australia and later New Zealand had growing security concerns as Pacific economies were increasingly becoming integrated into international processes of global connection (Hoadley, 2005). The term 'arc of instability' coined in the late 1990s to describe the Pacific arc 'from the Indonesian archipelago, East Timor and Papua New Guinea in the north, to the Solomon Islands, Vanuatu, Fiji, New Caledonia and New Zealand in the east' (Dibb, Hale & Prince, 1999, 18), turned a geographical descriptor into a strategic concept in Australian defence planning (Wallis, 2012). This characterisation of instability influenced political discourse in the region and provided a justification for interventionism (Wesley-Smith, 2007), particularly in the Western Pacific region referred as Melanesia. One example enacting a dramatic change in Australian policy post September 11 is the Regional Assistance Mission to Solomon Islands (RAMSI), which aimed to prevent a 'failing state' (Wainwright et al., 2003) seen as a threat for regional stability (Kabutaulaka, 2005).

Political concerns in New Zealand about migration and poverty in the Pacific can be traced back to the 1960s. Nonetheless, concerns linking a demographic youth bulge and unemployment in Melanesia started in the 1990s, given the increase in rural-urban mobility leading to urban squatter settlements in various Pacific countries (Hoadley, 2005). This move from rural dwellings to urban areas meant departing from an exclusive agrarian-based way of life. In several Pacific countries, moving to urban areas means relatives and extended families are relied upon for daily subsistence. Simultaneously, an increasing trend in youth unemployment had been building since the previous decades (AusAID, 2006; Ware, 2004). Trends in economic indicators, such as paid employment juxtaposed with demographic data on fertility and mortality rates, anticipated that a growing portion of the young population in the region urban areas would be unemployed in the coming decades, despite most young people in Pacific countries still live in rural areas.[12]

Coincidently, in the 1990s, there was an international reassessment of Western laissez faire policies which motivated analysts in New Zealand and Australia to record the 'apparently growing frequency and severity of poverty, corruption, crime, ethnic and secessionist violence, and military coups' (Hoadley, 2005, 6), particularly in Melanesia. Civil unrest and criminality were commonly associated with a significant proportion of young, male, and unemployed living in urban areas. Then, at the turn of the century, the South

---

[12] Besides Fiji and Kiribati where about 50 percent of their populations live in urban areas, the other Pacific countries have urbanization rates of around 20 percent.

Pacific was portrayed as needing a safety valve to prevent civil unrest and address the challenges of this diverse region (AusAID, 2006; Duncan, Chand, 2002; May, 2003; Ware, 2004; Ware, 2005). The body of knowledge produced before the RSE scheme was launched, through reports and conferences, emphasises the limitations of Pacific countries' governments and their local economies to cope with a youth bulge. Therefore, guaranteeing employment opportunities to reduce potential violence outbursts was the solution proposed to address existing security concerns, particularly for Melanesian countries, which had seen law and order incidents and violent conflicts since the 1980s and were depicted as suffering from weak governance and economic mismanagement (Kabutaulaka, 2015).

In 2006, the World Bank published a report, funded by the Australian government, which has been pivotal to the RSE scheme. This report conveyed institutionally endorsed recommendations and generated momentum for the launch of the scheme. Although authored by World Bank staff and consultants, 'Pacific Islands: At Home & Away' (World Bank, 2006) represents the formal opinion regarding labour mobility of the technical unit that produced it. This report portrays the increase in unemployment because of rural-urban migration and the increased urbanisation in Pacific countries emphatically tied to criminality and security. Young people were characterised as being behind the outbreaks of disorder, which was argued, were a factor in the low levels of investment in Pacific countries, and in turn impacted youth employment prospects, thus becoming victims of their own predicament. Acknowledging that Vanuatu data on aggregate employment does not provide a basis for projections of formal employment growth, this report uses GDP based trends as 'guesstimates of formal sector employment growth'[13] (World Bank, 2006, 35) to estimate the number of people that could potentially seek overseas employment. Therefore, the participation of ni-Vanuatu in the RSE scheme is questionable from a technical standpoint not only because of the lack of reliable data, but also because the underlying assumption of their unsuccessful transition away from a subsistence economy.

The 'young and the restless' (World Bank, 2006, 27) were made responsible for the existing insecurity in Pacific countries. This type of trope hides the root causes of development challenges or misrepresent them by portraying a vicious cycle maintained by unemployed young people. Such analyses disregard a variety of internal factors contributing to unemployment and the lack of local jobs because of limited economic growth in Pacific countries and the

---

[13] Similar calculations were made for the RSE scheme 'Big 3', Marshall Islands, and Papua New Guinea.

nature of such developments. For example, between the 1980s and 1990s, the decolonisation demands in New Caledonia, the Bougainville conflict, the Fiji coups, and Solomon Islands ethnic tensions, shifted attention to pressing issues (Kabutaulaka, 2015). Besides transferring the responsibility for their own unemployment, the insecurity situation in their countries, and other social problems to young people, little consideration was given to global forces such as the arrival of capitalism, Christianity, imperialism, part and parcel of processes of colonisation that have structured Pacific economies for centuries (Wesley-Smith, 1995). Particular values – part of a belittlement discourse towards Pacific peoples – also contribute to the moral characterisation of the youth bulge as restless.

Before the RSE scheme was designed, certain consensus was built among scholars and policy-makers in the region regarding the problems in the South Pacific, as evidenced in grey literature and in political speeches (Plimmer, 2006). From the acceptance of a 'culture of migration' in the region, to the analysis of push and pull factors (Bedford, R., 2006) to its potential positive impacts (Voigt-Graf, 2006) statistics and economic indicators were used to both confirm and articulate a mismatch between labour demand in New Zealand and labour supply in Pacific countries. The next section unfolds how labour mobility emerged as a solution to this problematisation and how young and unemployed men became subjects of governance in alignment with the global shift favouring temporary migration management policies and the underlying issues these programmes create.

3.2 Rectifying Problematic Demographics through Labour Mobility

The construction of the problems in the South Pacific region can be traced via a double discourse; a discourse on security originated in policy management discussions between the larger economies in the region, intertwined with a belittlement discourse towards their less developed neighbours (Hau'ofa, 1994; Kabutaulaka, 2015). These tropes contribute to laying the foundation for the management of migration by shaping the norms and forms applied to the international government of borders via interventionism (Andrijasevic, Walters, 2010). Proactive policies undertaken to prevent countries from becoming failed states can influence relationships among a state and its citizens.

Governmentality operates at different scales. At a macro level, international organisations can govern states and citizens through a number of techniques, including negotiations, consultancies, and contributing to pass national and international legislation and protocols (Loescher, 2001; Obokata, 2010; Vestergaard, 2009), while at the level of society, policies can govern the lived experiences of migrants and their communities through expert guidance. Unfolding the governmental aspects underlying the promotion of a cost-minimising solution to solve seasonal farming demands and simultaneously favour economic and socio-political stability in the region, is key to understand how foundational tropes are reified.

The success of governmental rationalities and their reification depend on a variety of factors beyond their discursive iteration and echoing by academic scholars and the official reports of international organisations. Rationalities are not necessarily systematic or closed, but they are 'morally coloured, grounded upon knowledge, and made thinkable through language' (Miller, Rose, 2008, 59), so that they can be adopted by a variety of epistemic communities. Political rationalities have a moral form, for example, when larger Pacific neighbours assume responsibilities for smaller ones. There is also a moral imperative driving the convergence of stakeholders' interests. Rationalities are organised upon authorities' duties addressing different actors' distribution of tasks and their epistemological character articulates them to some conception of the groups of objects or persons to be governed, such as the less developed neighbours and their remittances. Rationalities are also articulated in a distinctive idiom beyond just rhetoric, which renders reality amenable to political deliberations. New Zealand's relationship with its neighbours in the Pacific has for long been understood in a moral way, as there is a sense of responsibility of the larger economies over development in the region.

Pacific region scholars had argued that access to external opportunities for paid employment was crucial to preventing conflict, as creating new jobs would not be possible for Pacific economies on their own (Duncan, 2008; Ware, 2007). Thus, increases in unemployment rates could be prevented by providing access to labour markets in New Zealand and Australia (Bedford, R., 2008; Stahl, Appleyard, 2007) by opening the export of Pacific labour. Similarly, the World Bank, 'motivated by the need for jobs for the Pacific Islanders who cannot source them domestically' (World Bank, 2006, iii), had discussed seasonal migration and a variety of possible arrangements for temporary migration programmes, drawing on examples from other countries. Private sector representatives from the horticulture and viticulture sectors in New Zealand also stressed that accessing jobs through increased labour mobility was essential to their sector competitiveness in international markets. Because Pacific young people lacked skills, they fared worse in comparison to skilled workers, who in theory had more employment options. Temporary labour mobility for unskilled youth was thus a favoured and convenient solution. It could alleviate the pressure on Pacific governments to develop their citizens' skills or increase their access to education, traditionally considered as the way to mitigate unemployment (Booth, 1994). New Zealand's policies, already encouraged stratified long and short-term migration. The then Department of Labour and Immigration New Zealand (INZ), already granted work rights, classified occupations, and designated essential skills to respond to labour shortages.

South Pacific politicians had been advocating for labour mobility before the signing of the Pacific Agreement on Closer Economic Relations (PACER) in 2001. The PACER committed to integrating labour markets and labour mobility, considered a central element for economic integration between the PIF countries and Australia and New Zealand (Noonan, 2011). The Pacific Plan, aimed to strengthen and deepen regional cooperation and integration, included labour mobility as a component of the economic growth pillar in the 2005 Kalibobo Roadmap. Labour mobility was one of the twenty-four initiatives identified for immediate implementation between 2005 and 2014, with the key objective of '... improved income earnings and livelihoods through better access to goods, services, employment and other development opportunities. The Plan includes initiatives for better access to markets and goods, trade in services including labour ...' (PIFS, 2005a, 9). Temporary movement of labour for the unskilled was subsequently included in the PICTA and the Economic Partnerships Agreement (EPA) (Maclellan, Mares, 2006). These discussions were also shifting away from deploying international development aid in alignment with the 2005 Paris Declaration on Aid Effectiveness, which proposed changes to aid provision.

Labour mobility through the RSE scheme was proposed as one solution to unemployment and insecurity which would expand job opportunities for unskilled Pacific Islanders and meet peak time agricultural labour needs. Given the number of workers initially considered, it was expected to complement other migration initiatives in the region.[14] The rationalities underpinning the scheme capitalise on the special relationship that New Zealand has with Pacific countries from its earlier colonial ties, and because of its domestic and international economic and political interests. The moral understanding of these relationships entails a sense of responsibility for development in the region to transform the so-called arc of instability into an arc of responsibility (Dobell, 2012; Wallis, 2012). However, because Pacific states were constituted during colonial times, they were never states in a Western sense and thus not prone to falling apart or failing in the way feared by New Zealand and Australia. In the Pacific, colonial divisions overlaid traditional indigenous social and political organisation (Wesley-Smith, 2007) and so a Western-style model of state was never consolidated. Nonetheless, the choice of labour mobility was plausible

---

[14] While the cap for RSE workers has almost quadrupled, current concerns are due to the compound effects on Pacific labour markets due to the large number of Pacific workers temporarily migrating to Australia under a similar scheme.

because international migration was considered less dependent on Pacific economies than on the destination countries.

3.3 Regulations Governing Labour Mobility

The moral imperative to assist Pacific countries' development is evident in the idiom underpinning the RSE scheme. The development narrative capitalises on the 'special relationship' that New Zealand has with the Pacific, providing an 'historical–ideological explanation' for the choice of labour pools (Barker, 2010). Once different bodies of knowledge constructed socioeconomic problems of Pacific countries in a cognitively plausible and simplified way, the basis for designing solutions was set and acted upon. In this case, the problem was defined in terms of economic costs, thus the solution was to open the borders to newcomers offering them pay within industry ranges. Whereas if the problem had been defined in terms of labour market outcomes, other solutions could have been raising sectoral wages and earnings domestically, reducing the occupational health impacts of agriculture, or removing other barriers discouraging locals' engagement in agricultural labour.

A top down approach is evident in the RSE scheme design, from international organisations governing states by delineating the characteristics of national migration policies, providing expert advice, and through more institutionalised means such as the Toso Vaka o Manū. This New Zealand government programme tailored to accompany the scheme aims to build organisational skills in Pacific governments' officials, expected to learn foreign models to manage migration. Based on the monitoring of performance measures and periodically collected data, areas of improvement are identified to further educational trainings on the matters at stake. This is indicative of how new problematisation gives room for adjustments and better management, creating successive cycles of new problems to be solved (Miller, Rose, 2008). Expert advice is also reflected in guidelines, checklists, and other practical instruments used to operationalise the scheme.

The RSE scheme relies on bilateral agreements that outline the conditions and the distribution of tasks for different countries' stakeholders. These interagency understandings emphasise restrictions for foreign workers and have a strong focus on obligations, the importance of compliance, and work ethics during pre-departure briefings (MFAT, 2007). Employers are governed through operational manuals (INZ, 2010) which regulate their conduct when dealing with workers, introducing changes regarding the provision of accommodation, pastoral care, and other matters that do not affect the hiring of other temporary workers, such as holidaymakers (backpackers) or New Zealanders (Tipples, Rawlinson, 2014). The private sector meets government conditions when applying for RSE status, complying with employment laws, providing suitable accommodation and pastoral care to guarantee workers' guidance and support during their stay. Finally, applicants to the scheme meet immigration requirements, including good character, health (testing negative for TBC and HIV/AIDS) and medical insurance acceptance criteria.

To be able to manage the wellbeing of populations it is important to define who belongs to it. The creation of this temporary scheme defines the criteria to govern certain groups of Pacific peoples, namely the young, unemployed, and semi-skilled. The representation of what is to be governed entails a technical process to transform phenomena into information, such as nature of work (i.e. skilled or unskilled) and labour needs. The collection of this information is not neutral, but a way of devising techniques to make the domain in question subject to evaluation, calculation, and intervention (Miller, Rose, 2008). For example, the classification of skills and how they are paid, assigns a market value to quantified labour, which is ultimately factored in business profits. For example, employers can decide paying hourly or piece rates to encourage productivity.

Potential RSE scheme participants become productive and entrepreneurial subjects to distinguish themselves from the unemployed by improving their employability. This implies they need to be educated to function as good workers employable in a Western economy. In doing so, they learn practical skills and adapt their behaviour to the offered labour conditions. In comparison to aid, it has been argued migration requires prospective migrants' major attitudinal changes so they can self-select to migrate (Curtain et al., 2016). Considering migrants as resources to be tapped (Brinkerhoff, 2008) in terms of remittances, and making them responsible for the development of their communities encourages their uptake of such transformations. Workers become 'the correlative of a governmentality which systematically changes the variables of the "environment" and can count on the "rational choice" of the individuals' (Lemke, 2001, 200) who respond to the conditions established for their subsistence. Thus, migration becomes a matter of choice rather than a necessity (Piper, 2009) but it is not exempt from costs. Due to these transformations, individuals assume the risks and responsibilities of their entrepreneurial activities and their potential failure.

The circularity of seasonal migration guarantees that participants do not fully leave their countries of origin. Instead, to deal with their predicaments, workers are turned into positive and responsible agents of change. Remittances, knowledge transfer, and the creation of businesses and trade networks could undoubtedly bring change, thus the emphasis on quantifying material outcomes of the RSE scheme over the years. The flow of remittances is expected to encourage development activities in workers' own communities and economic development for their country as a whole. At this point, the justification of the RSE scheme as a neutral economic development solution suddenly dissipates, as the political, social and economic responsibility for development is placed on the shoulders of workers. This responsibility does not even fall to the sending countries' governments, but rather on those who produce the economic benefits and personally assume its costs. As some recent studies have shown (Bedford, C., Bedford, R. & Nunns, 2020; Nunns, Bedford, C. & Bedford, R., 2019) assuming this responsibility can deprive rural communities of a large percentage of their working age population[15] and of their contributions to their subsistence resulting in elevated social costs (Petrou, Connell, 2023b).

3.4 The Neoliberal Underpinnings of the 'Triple Win' Narrative

As explained, in Section 1.4, the 'triple win' narrative is a constitutive feature of current migration management programmes. Its origins can be traced to IOM's guide for policy-makers (2004) which supports voluntary and orderly migration for the benefit of all stakeholders involved. The RSE scheme was designed based on the Canadian Seasonal Agricultural Worker Program (SAWP) in alignment with its temporary migration model (Ramasamy et al., 2008). Under this logic, developing countries opt for labour opportunities in developed countries where there is an objective and measurable statistical mismatch of labour demand and supply. In this way, the labour needs of countries of origin and destination are linked. Destination countries can address labour shortages through temporary migration, while individuals are incentivised by monetary gains to temporarily migrate to sell their labour.

Proposing the RSE scheme as a 'triple win' solution aligned neatly with the interests of its different stakeholders. First, the private sector had been lobbying their government for a solution to secure a labour force required at peak harvest, packing, and pruning seasons. Second, the New Zealand Government aimed 'to support economic growth and productivity of the industry as a whole' and 'to encourage economic development, regional integration and good governance within the Pacific' (INZ, 2010). Shortly after its inception, the scheme was considered a model for fair recruitment and policy coherence (Whatman, van Beek, 2008) due to New Zealand's domestic policy impacts on the development

---

[15] An analysis combining the absence of workers due to the RSE scheme in New Zealand and the SWP in Australia identified that 52.5% of Tongan men aged 20–29 were away from their rural communities for most part of the 2018/19 agricultural season (Bedford, C., Bedford R. & Nunns, 2020). If this figure is compounded with the migration for trade and professional training, which also requires long absences, the result is even more dramatic. Almost a quarter of ni-Vanuatu working aged men were absent during the same period.

outcomes of participant developing countries, and because it promoted regional labour mobility (ILO, 2015). The participatory approach taken by policymakers working on a Medium-Long-Term Horticulture and Viticulture Seasonal Labour Strategy paved the way for the RSE scheme, resonating with the interests of the main stakeholders involved (OECD, 2014). Finally, Pacific countries, which had historically advocated for access to larger labour markets considered the scheme as an opportunity to widen employment options for unskilled workers.

During the first decade of the RSE scheme it received a positive characterisation in the mainstream arguing it achieved the 'elusive triple wins' for which it was designed (IMSED Research, 2010; McKenzie, Gibson, 2014) improving prospects for employment, increasing remittances, and stabilising fragile states (World Bank, 2017). However, the 'triple win' scenario is contradicted by the operationalisation of the RSE scheme and its purported neutrality by the highly unequal sharing of gains, which have largely contributed to benefit the horticulture and viticulture sectors in New Zealand (Bedford, C. Bedford, R. & Nunns, 2020). The reliance on workers' remittances to promote development, as articulated in the 'triple win' argument, was based on a purely notional cost–benefit analysis (Ramasamy et al., 2008). Arguably, this initial analysis presents relatively similar benefits for the involved parties, shifting attention away from any potential imbalances in the wins or loses; or from the conditions under which they are produced, as if the presumed end of development justifies the means used to achieve it.

In the following section, the specific case from Vanuatu, a country that relies on a semi-subsistence economy, challenges the dominant 'triple win' narrative through the manifestation of medium and long-term social impacts of the scheme. Without intending to diminish the economic and material achievements of New Zealand companies and RSE workers, the next section builds on the existing criticism of the unequivocal relationship between labour migration and development and the 'triple win' solution it arguably offers (Basok, Piper & Simmons, 2013; Basok, Bélanger, 2016; Underhill-Sem et al., 2019; Wickramasekara, 2011). Globally, temporary migration programmes perpetuate inequalities between countries and the vulnerability of migrant workers within the North–South divide. The focus on the relations produced by policies and practices at an individual scale, aims to contribute to the discussion of how the RSE scheme fits in the lives of Pacific peoples rather than how them fit in a 'development intervention'.

4 Winners and Losers: Transforming Subjectivities

Paying attention to the lived experiences and worldviews of migrants, elucidates the complex negotiations they undergo to engage in seasonal migration. Globally, circular migration managers are becoming more aware about the implications that the push for development can have for the lives of people moving temporarily outside their home country borders, and realising how national policies impact day-to-day lived experiences, particularly after COVID. Beyond the broader international factors and national concerns that underpinned the launch of the RSE scheme, a relational analysis brings a distinct dimension to understand the governance of regional mobility. This critical view towards approaches concerned with populations often hide the materiality of personal experiences and individuals social relations which cannot be expressed in figures. This research is grounded on fieldwork carried out with ni-Vanuatu, their families and members of their communities, as well as with pastoral care workers and Vakameasina tutors.

The transformations encouraged by this temporary form of employment are described, avowing the mobility of workers and their absence in their communities as a condition for the 'wins' they return with, such as money, skills, values, and status. At the same time, ambiguous wins and losses, result from relational changes and the forging of new labour, family, and community relations. To facilitate the analysis of the hierarchies operating in the scheme, two main authority groups are differentiated. Authority figures; namely, the employers, pastoral care workers, and team leaders in New Zealand, and local authorities such as village chiefs, pastors, church and other community members in Vanuatu. When referring to individuals, is to highlight neoliberal subjectivation processes, as I intentionally avoid engaging with the conceptualisations of personhood ascribed to Melanesians. How social relations are intertwined and how their effects are amplified across borders, can be appreciated when village members exercise power over relations outside their territory through team leaders and workers, and employers influence social relations in Vanuatu villages, allowing for a multidirectional exercise of power that produces new subjectivities.

The analysis of how self-care and discipline transform conducts in spaces of regulated freedom (Rose, 1999) highlights how norms adjust and adapt individuals to certain behavioural standards habituating their choices. Such techniques take form in strategies, tactics and ways of thinking and acting used in governing 'for the benefit' of Pacific peoples to increase incomes, and promote 'development'. Specific forms of governmentality, techniques, and rationalities produce specific subjectivities and forms of knowledge, to which specific forms of self-control integrate. The neoliberal rationalities underpinning the RSE scheme construct productive subjects and entrepreneurial selves through discipline, making 'individuals behave, to be efficient and productive workers' (Foucault, 2003, 239). Politically obedient individuals – the good workers – become a requirement for an economically productive population. Thus, for the RSE scheme to

Development Subjectivities and Governmentality

continue, a specific knowledge of its functioning needs to be transferred to its different stakeholders to voluntarily engage in labour mobility.

4.1 Improving Standards of Living through a Development Idiom

The neoliberal rationalities underpinning the RSE scheme have been articulated with local rationalities and customary worldviews, to stress the importance of people having an opportunity to become employed, earn money, and use this money to help themselves and their families. These narratives transform workers' subjectivities over the course of their engagement with the scheme. In understanding the social domain as economic, new forms of knowledge convey that workers have to be at the same time responsible and moral, and economic-rational individuals (Lemke, 2001). This section analyses the knowledge underlying the conception of what is good, productive, efficient, or profitable, as framed by the RSE scheme regulations, their interpretation and operationalisation by its main stakeholders.

Several instances from recruitment to return, inform workers of development expectations, placing strong emphasis on money and savings. Different government stakeholders use development tropes as an idiom. During pre-departure trainings, which span few hours in sending countries' Labour Management Units, participants complete the paperwork to have their visa processed and receive instructions and recommendations about what to expect regarding work and the costs of living while working in New Zealand. The 'Get Ready' video (Settlement Support New Zealand, 2011), a training tool developed with the support of various New Zealand and Pacific government agencies is tailored to each participant country. It explains details of the scheme with messages that emphasise how workers' money is spent: 'The main reason for you to come to New Zealand is to make money to send to your family or to take it back with you to Vanuatu [...] Suppose you want to save a lot of money; you must exercise control [...] Your employer can help you save money with one separate bank account' (2011, 10:30).[16] It also encourages self-control to be able to return home with earnings, and the boundaries of certain behaviours to achieve the desired development.

Team leaders with the same development idiom, reinforce messages to restrict consumption while in New Zealand and to use earnings for better purposes, such as building permanent houses, often depicted as 'better houses'.[17] Few ni-Vanuatu had experienced an employer-employee relationship

---

[16] Free translation from Bislama.
[17] Smith (2018) analysed the social transformations brought by the construction of new houses and the apparent shift from reciprocal community-based lifestyles towards nuclear families.

before their engagement in the RSE scheme,[18] as most did not have paid employment. Besides their work in subsistence agriculture through gardening, some had relied on churches or earned cash through sporadic work opportunities. Money was incorporated in economic terms, as a symbol of status, and a means to obtain non-material benefits, which seem to have created new notions of merit (Cummings, 2013a). Workers demonstrate they are good kinsmen and providers by attending to the needs of their families and having the strength to endure the separation and the hard agricultural work. In contrast, for the ones who are not invited back to New Zealand, staying in Vanuatu is often associated with economic failure or even personal catastrophe, as will be later explained.

Even as some ni-Vanuatu identified themselves as RSE workers, some did not identify their labour as a source of income. This can prevent a proper understanding of the transactions implied in contract relationships and their implication for workers' rights and obligations as New Zealand taxpayers. Instead, they related work to aid and the good-will of New Zealanders giving them money they otherwise cannot access, or considered their work as a reciprocal gift (Smith, 2019). One worker explained: 'New Zealand helps a lot, gives good, gives good money to Vanuatu [...] That is the good thing of New Zealand, they are helping out the ni-Vanuatu with their needs. That's why we come all here, work, get money and get back. Just to help us fill up our standard of our living.' (oral communication, Vincent, team leader, 7th RSE season, Hawke's Bay, 01-06-2014). These earnings will help achieve a different – not necessarily better – status (Smith, 2018) and will also bring important cultural changes.

The expectations of the villages and church congregations can also reinforce conformity with the conditions of the RSE scheme. Churches are often part of participants' support networks and there is a strong sense of obligation towards them. Workers' contributions to community projects can also be highly valued, especially if represented as voluntary gifts (Smith, 2021). As most workers are Christians, adherence to said values and religious services attendance is encouraged. Religion is entangled in traditional worldviews and blends with other aspects of ni-Vanuatu lives, with church hierarchies influencing ranking practices, and personal qualities of priests and pastors becoming equivalent to that of chiefs (Jolly, 2012). In sum, the idiom of development fosters new practices, discriminating good from bad workers, according to prescribed behaviours. It functions as a

---

[18] When the scheme started only 48 percent of workers had ever had a paid job (McKenzie, D., Garcia Martinez & Winters et al., 2008), around 30 percent of participants in this research had sporadic jobs.

disciplinary mechanism in that employers, governments, team leaders, and workers transform their conduct with both empowering and disempowering effects.

4.2 Gaining Ground? New Leadership and Notions of Merit

The transformations of ni-Vanuatu participating in the RSE scheme can have both empowering and disempowering effects. New hierarchies being forged have accommodated existing ones, but can also be resisted and contested. The authority team leaders exercise over workers in New Zealand can also be reproduced to a certain extent in their home countries. This is reminiscent of the social and cultural changes encouraged by labour trade returnees in the Nineteenth century, who challenged hierarchies, and became instrumental in Christian conversions and Christianism incorporation to local values (Jolly, 2012; Rio, 2019). Nonetheless, when company workers belong to the same community, learning different ways to relate can be challenging. The shift from relating as colleague to relating as members of the same or a neighbouring village back home can become onerous, as daily interactions are coloured by past experiences, for example relations become tense if work-related grievances have been ignored. Mobility is desired and managed according to participants' own ability to access existing channels, thus, networks cannot be broken. The experiences of previous travellers also play a significant role in shaping ni-Vanuatu subjectivities.

Team leaders are authority figures credited as one of the factors for the success of the RSE scheme (Bailey, 2017). Workers are grouped under the supervision of a leader who is in charge of resolving day-to-day issues and liaising with employers. In large companies, several leaders can be in charge of the same group, and their politics have the potential of transforming livelihoods. It is generally assumed that leaders can easily interact with workers to explain things in their own words and language, thus both employers and pastoral care workers rely heavily on them. However, this depends on leaders' character and how comfortable they are in their role. While being well-versed in local customary practices, not all leaders have a complete understanding of practical matters such as wage deductions or additional payments. Some consider they should not bother employers and try to do their best with the information at hand before requesting a meeting to clarify workers' questions. Others are fearful of raising workers grievances, which can negatively influence the welfare of the whole group.

The background of team leaders is diverse, some are pastors, village chiefs, or those with more schooling who already had a privileged status in their communities.

But complete schooling is not a requirement, leaders can be selected because of their ability to speak English, their active participation in meetings, or their good relationship with authorities. Others are chosen because of their respected role in their communities. Pastors use a religious discourse to facilitate workers' acceptance of their role. When religion – or biblical references – are used to legitimise leaders' role, they are less likely to be challenged. On occasions, leaders conveyed bible verses related to good and evil or to reaping and sowing to encourage responsibility and productivity. Ni-Vanuatu often perceive spiritual power connected with both the material and immaterial worlds (Jolly, 2012), thus attuned with the prosperity gospel they could foresee the consequences of their actions. In other instances, team leaders could be considered as having a similar status to village chiefs,[19] although this is often contested.

Workers within the same company can become team leaders at different points in time. When workers are made temporary leaders of a smaller group, such as the leader of the bedroom, portacom, or camper van where they sleep, they change their behaviour to assure their group complies with expectations. In this way, workers cannot longer complain because their role had changed. One worker noted: 'Everyone is a leader here' (oral communication, Percy, 4th RSE season, Hawke's Bay, 01-03-2015) as he and others were given said role to prevent complaints. He described how colleagues were named as leaders of a room, to ensure others are ready to timely depart for work, keep their room clean, clean themselves, and take their turns at cooking. These unofficial team leaders did not believe their status was real because, unlike the team leader who appointed them, they had no direct connection with their employer. This disciplining strategy was sometimes used to reduce grievances, while at the same time increased accountability in the group. In sum, discipline regulates the conduct of workers, as leaders represent employer's interests in ensuring that everyone gets to work, eats, goes to sleep on time, and complies with existing rules.

The status bestowed empowers leaders beyond the workplace, influencing workers during their free time in New Zealand, and by extension in their home countries; for example by getting more involved in village affairs when returning home, despite not previously having such a role. In one of the villages visited, a RSE scheme worker born to the current chief, was in line to assume the chiefdom, but it had been offered to his team leader. In those villages, chiefdom

---

[19] Vanuatu maintains systems of chiefdom, which vary depending on place, from graded societies in Northern and Central Vanuatu to inherited, rank-based or due to influence and obligations. The polities in rural Vanuatu are not centralised and chiefs intervene in local communities' decisions built on obligations and counter-obligations.

was usually inherited, though in nearby regions chiefs could also be nominated. This offer was contentious as some community members preferred to adhere to what was customarily prescribed, while others questioned the nominee's lack of consideration for workers' needs while in New Zealand, which would be unacceptable for becoming a chief. Conflicts are produced when priorities not established at village level change. New forms of authority and new skills such as demonstrating prowess to succeed in the scheme can become more valued than traditional ones, and can be considered deserving of a chiefdom, instead of customary ways. Bailey (2017) argues this is due to non-traditional leaders' social capital gains, which speaks of the increasing reliance on mobilising local networks for development. The broader transformations brought by a neoliberal rationality could have contradictory implications changing the understanding of merit and transforming social practices in relation to chieftaincy.

Employers also influence workers' understanding of merit. In the media, sectoral communications and in the materials used during the pre-departure trainings (Settlement Support New Zealand, 2011), RSE scheme workers' productivity is often compared to other non-RSE scheme workers. Comparisons to New Zealanders are often made in terms of productivity, although it seems their expectations regarding the availability of jobs are misaligned (IMSED Research, 2010), as not enough domestic workers are willing to engage on agricultural work at the pay level offered, or working conditions do not meet their expectations (Basok, 2002; Sharma, 2006). Whatever the case, the productivity message reinforces the good worker image that workers aim to embody.

4.3 A Penny Saved Is a Penny Earned

Money management is strongly governed in the RSE scheme, from voluntary savings initiatives[20] led by companies/employers to prevent 'wasteful spending,' to leaders' advice regarding money use, and churches requesting contributions. While ni-Vanuatu lived experiences are unique they are also influenced by their age, sex, parenthood, marital status among other intersecting identities; thus money management will depend on families' priorities such as building a more permanent house or paying for children's education. During my fieldwork, most young ni-Vanuatu workers considered being told too often to make 'good use' of money. Community members and workers characterised individuals spending their money in New Zealand as young or immature, not knowing

---

[20] During my fieldwork, some employers withheld a share of workers' salaries and gave workers an 'advance' to cover weekly expenses.

what they were doing, and even calling them 'crazy' because their behaviour did not meet commonplace expectations.

Differences in RSE scheme workers' aspirations are also mediated by the conditions in their home countries (Bedford, C., Bedford R. & Nunns, 2020). In the case of countries prone to cyclones, one of the main goals is to build a house made of concrete. Workers set time-bound goals for the accomplishment of material achievements such as buying land, or construction materials, and sometimes their participation in the scheme depends on the completion of their houses; as they plan to stop travelling once construction finishes. Team leaders' encouragement can lead to them establishing clear requirements and periodically verifying that workers are meeting goals, despite this can make them unpopular. Co-workers and family members are critical of spending in activities considered unproductive, and warn this may cause family separations: 'Some people when they get there, they do not manage them[selves] properly . . . some they want to go to town, buy all the stuff, or even drink alcohol, sometimes they spend their money now without thinking of their families back home.' (oral communication, Heilene, team leader's wife, Efate, 03-11-2014). A worker who engaged in the scheme since the first season criticised colleagues who: 'just played up with their money here in New Zealand, when they go home they have no money, and sometimes they have to divorce their wives [. . .] they didn't look after them because of the money, they misused the moneys [. . .] when they go home some of them, they divorce their families, their wives and children. That's very bad.' (oral communication, Betty, 6th RSE season, Hawke's Bay, 01-06-2014). There is strong peer pressure to conform to the acceptable behaviours.

The RSE scheme income also funds primary and secondary education for ni-Vanuatu own or extended family's children. The expectation of achieving better lives and jobs to support their families in the long run is placed on higher educational attainment. While workers expect their children to benefit from 'better futures', it was unclear how they reconcile these aspirations with traditional roles and responsibilities towards their local communities. The repeated parental absences can also result in children's increased household responsibilities, losing important resilience skills, and having increased material expectations that could make them disregard a traditional communal life. It appears that the influx of money is transforming traditional practices such as communal work (Craven, 2015; Rockell, 2015), childcare (Rohorua et al., 2009), gardening and house building (Smith, 2016; Smith, 2021), as this can now be paid for or delegated to others. The relational changes money influx produces may not be noticeable in communities closer to urban centres or until they have acquired a more definitive form, though to a certain extent, these can be appreciated by researchers returning to Vanuatu after some years.

Social practices around subsistence gardening are being transformed due to the availability of money. Less labour intensive crops are planted, and temporary workers are hired to take care of specific tasks such as weeding, planting or harvesting when family members are absent but also after their return. While this is mostly valued by RSE scheme workers' families, these transactions could signal withdrawal from former communal work (Smith, 2018). Other migrants from the global south face similar experiences when leaving behind their own social reproduction roles and domestic responsibilities in their home countries, to migrate for waged income. Excluding basic social reproduction aspects in a semi-subsistence economy poses challenges to the villages, as productive community members are absent for months at a time, often for half a year. The culture surrounding mobility and stories of resilience and success behind the RSE scheme, as one of the most prominent labour mobility development programmes (McKenzie, Gibson, 2014) to be copied and exported, muted for a long time the voices of participants and their families. Some participants complained about children not being able to recognise their fathers when looking at them on arrival.

The use of money is associated with techniques of self-care, because workers have to learn to control themselves to save their income for the common good. This self-control is specific and instrumental to the objective of positive remittance flows and contrasts with a more liberal approach by which individuals could freely allocate their income. The emphasis on development gains generates a set of measures that no other temporary workers in New Zealand have in place to control their spending, such as the savings schemes set up by employers. The normalisation of the productive investment of remittances encourage ni-Vanuatu to become entrepreneurial subjects. One example of the institutionalisation of entrepreneurship is the Yumi Growem Vanuatu initiative launched in 2021, which explicitly aims to re-shape returned workers' lives by growing individuals' confidence and shaping their way of thinking. This initiative is fully funded by the governments of Australia and New Zealand to capitalise on remittances and deliver governments' goals (V-labs, 2021). These entrepreneurial subjectivities reinforce a neoliberal understanding of welfare, based on individuals being made responsible for their own wellbeing, whereby remittances allow families to pay for education, household, and communal infrastructure.

4.4 Entrepreneurs of Themselves? Governing Productivity

Productivity is a feature of economic government aligned with a neoliberal rationality, as populations are disciplined with the aim of safeguarding and increasing their productivity. This discipline extends to time management, as repetition and circularity involve workers in new processes of subjectivation. Discipline as a technique creates physical routines that enable workers to become more productive and to achieve their planned development goals. Some leaders encouraged groups to work faster to get more money each week, and in turn workers complained, as they felt more tired each time. It is implicitly assumed, though some workers are constantly reminded of it, that performance improvements make their participation in subsequent seasons more probable. Just as it is difficult for workers to contest the development argument, the economic and social benefits of commodifying ni-Vanuatu labour across borders reinforce Pacific countries decision to continue their engagement with the scheme.

The fact that it is usually the most productive workers who are retained for following seasons speaks to the techniques operating to govern labour mobility. The instruments used to manage productivity are timetables on the employers' side and workers' paystubs on the leaders' side. However, these same paystubs can be used by workers as instruments for grievances recognition (Street, 2012), for example, when they contest deductions. Disciplinary mechanisms are not unidirectional. Transportation deductions are often contested, as costs are higher for RSE workers from the same company who work far away from where they are lodged, because they do not have a say on the location of the orchard they are assigned to. In the case of companies that transfer workers between New Zealand's North and South Island, charges for bus and ferry affect workers' seasonal earnings. The more experienced workers are aware of how they can maximise their earnings, and also of their employers' attempts to maximise profits and reduce losses aiming for efficiency gains. Introducing rosters for cleaning and cooking in smaller groups facilitates better use of resources such as power and cleaning supplies. Although workers are not always satisfied being the last group to cook and eat, team leaders make sure this system works without major disruptions.

The link between good character and employability is strengthened when becoming return workers, as they have proven to be reliable, hard-working, and well-behaved in conforming to the requirements of working and living in New Zealand (ESU, 2014). In contrast, participants whose names were not on the employer's returnees' list, will be singled out because of having lost such an opportunity. Workers not asked to return have not been necessarily sanctioned, they may be poor performers or they may also be asked to return later (Smith, 2019). However, the tropes regarding banning and blacklisting, discussed in the next section, will shape how communities perceive non-returning participants, as they have failed to make good use of an opportunity for their own improvement. Workers' reputation, good standing, and social status in the village are at stake.

Grounded in the knowledge of the ideal characteristics of participants in the scheme, workers are valued because of their employability, which is reflected in their ability to become a return worker. Nonetheless, luck continues to be a common explanation allowing individuals to distance themselves from a negative outcome.

As in any workplace, conflicts arise from different sources. Some interviewees noted that they earn less than New Zealanders despite their hard work and productivity. Sometimes, employers averaged out earnings to meet the minimum hours requirement of their RSE status (Bedford, C., Bedford, R. & Nunns, 2020) which may increase confusion regarding a biased treatment. During my fieldwork, contrary to the pay gap that contract work often entails for women, female workers in one company initially earned more than males, as both were earning the same wage although there was a difference in the number of hours worked. This was perceived as unfair for men, whose working hours depended on the weather and piece rates and involved more demanding physical work, driving leaders to negotiate a solution with their employer. Work related tensions are also dealt with humour. Sometimes, workers show respect in public or in the presence of strangers, but joke in private. Resistance to leaders' decisions can take the form of questioning, keeping secrets, or ignoring their advice. Workers had also questioned leaders' selection if it seems arbitrary to them. Nonetheless, hardly any workers ask upfront questions or publicly criticise official guidelines or discretionary rules.

Living together as a group, having to manage their own time for the sake of productivity, can imply waking up and going to bed at specific times, not watching movies or content not approved by leaders, not engaging in recreational sports to reduce the risk of injuries, and ultimately avoiding anything which could negatively impact their ability to work. Such prohibitions and behavioural guidelines are controversial, and often boundaries regarding the activities allowed while in New Zealand are not clear. Despite regulations define minimum requirements to be met by employers, their discretion is commonplace, and workers' understanding of what is acceptable varies across companies. The operationalisation of sanctions is articulated to enable workers to direct their energies to their work. Participants are encouraged to comply with unofficial but accepted practices. They have persuaded themselves to produce informed behaviours that will allow them to succeed. Being a good worker goes beyond just being productive, it entails behaving well during and in between contracts so as not to jeopardise an upcoming season (Bedford, C., Bedford, R & Nunns, 2020; Cummings, 2013a; Rockell, 2015). The problematisation of becoming unemployed and being idle implies activities which do not use time wisely, such as walking around, are considered undesirable (Smith, 2016) and unproductive and can thus be punished. This raises concerns with the underlying assumptions that legitimise the transformations of workers' relations in their communities.

4.5 No Harm, No Foul? Sanctioning Misbehaviour

Governmental techniques are not exclusively related to the state as various modes of authority are not unidirectional, but governments can institutionalise sanctions. Institutionalised mechanisms to sanction workers who do not behave according to expected standards are not exclusive to Vanuatu. When discipline becomes institutionalised, it is possible to identify the relations between the governmental techniques that produce certain behaviours at the individual level. This section aims to interrogate the objectives pursued, the types of conduct targeted, and the techniques used. Quality standards' definitions used by Pacific governments are not an arbitrary adaptation of labour codes and regulations, but respond to different stakeholders' interests. Defining what misconduct and misdemeanours entail have led to the application of stand-downs, banning, and blacklisting. Guaranteeing workers' rights is one of the purported benefits of migration management, nonetheless, the institutionalisation of sanctioning practices, is de facto leading to the erosion of workers' rights and can affect entire communities.

A measure taken by the Vanuatu Department of Labour Employment Services Unit (ESU) to penalise workers reported by their leaders, or employer representatives, for 'tarnishing Vanuatu's reputation in New Zealand or Australia' (ESU, 2013, 1) is the compilation of lists. The ESU separates stand-down and ban lists and the decision to place a worker on either of them depends on the Department of Labour in consultation with their New Zealand RSE scheme counterparts. Up to 2019, to minimise 'the risk of an unsuitable person being selected for RSE/SWP' (ESU, 2013, 2) these lists were circulated to recruiters. Thereafter, recruiters must check with the ESU before applying for visas (ESU, 2019), as lists are no longer publicly available. Workers can be on stand-down for their misconduct in seasonal programmes from one to five seasons depending on the nature and seriousness of the offense. If workers are reinstated after 'serving their penalty', their names are removed from the ESU managed dataset, though if reinstated workers misbehave following an earlier stand-down, they automatically receive a permanent ban. In an effort to compete with other countries, the government of Vanuatu has also defined quality standards for RSE workers including productivity, work ethic, good character, manageability, health, and capacity to cope, being role models, and demonstrating adequate English communication (ESU, 2019).

The ESU guide on sanctions (ESU, 2013) created with the support of international consultants, prescribes permanent bans from labour mobility schemes in serious cases. Some changes and additional clauses were added to the 2019 Migrant Labour Disciplinary Policy (ESU, 2019). Poor productivity and other misbehaviours, including failure to board a flight are penalised with one to two years stand-down; and damage to property, repeated difficult to manage misbehaviour (formerly disruptive, uncooperative behaviour), with a stand-down between three to four years. In 2013, fighting, consumption of alcohol or drugs, and sexual harassment were punishable by a five-year stand-down. In 2019, having affairs, abusing alcohol, using drugs, and being sent home by the employer were also penalised with a stand-down of five years, while sexual assault replaced sexual harassment in this time bracket. Finally, in 2013, dishonesty, theft, sexual or physical assault and involvement with the New Zealand or Australian Police or Courts led to a permanent ban, while in 2019, fraud and falsification, and drunk driving were added as causals for banning workers permanently. Reasons for the reduction of the penalty for sexual assault, from a permanent ban in 2013 to a five-year stand-down period in 2019 are unknown, given that no regulatory change in Vanuatu penal code took place after 2006, when sections dealing with sexual intercourse without consent and abduction were amended.[21]

Being blacklisted is the term commonly used when workers have to stand-down or are banned from the RSE scheme, and individual cases are often used as an example. One woman told me crying 'so many of my friends, they have been called and they [leaders] banned them and I don't want them to do that. A friend from my company, friends of mine, my colleagues [...] maybe ten of them [...] very sad.' (oral communication, Berenice, 3rd RSE season, Efate, 15-10-2014). While the ESU guide on sanctions refers to establishing the validity of any reports against workers, allegations can be based on hearsay. In some cases, there is only the word of the worker against that of the leader, who has more credibility as an authority. New Zealand labour regulations stipulate that in the interest of fairness and reasonableness, employers have an obligation to advise their employees in the event of misconduct that a warning may follow. If there is an issue of serious misconduct, the employer must advise the employee that their employment may be at risk, and a dismissal can be justified following a disciplinary investigation. However, sometimes investigations are not undertaken (NZHRC, 2022) but leaders' trusted advice can determine who is invited to return the following season.

---

[21] A 2016 Amendment in the Penal code extends its scope to protect minors.

New Zealand government officers argued that they respect decisions made by Pacific governments as sovereign nations. In doing so, both sending and receiving governments have empowered employers and team leaders to exercise their discretion without considering existing legal Acts[22] in place that prohibit fraudulent employment practices. The scheme is subject to the New Zealand Employment Relations Act (2000) which protects workers and allows employers' discretion, for example, defining the number and distribution of breaks over the working day. Critics of the latest Employment Relations Amendment Act note it prioritises business needs over the employees' well-being (Wilson, M. A., 2014). More recently, an analysis of the RSE scheme has uncovered potential human rights violations (NZHRC, 2022).

Prior to 2013, much more discretion was used to determine sanctions. Guidelines and additional structure for the scheme management were supported by the World Bank and the Pacific Cooperation Foundation's 'Institutional Capacity Building for Labour Export in the Pacific' project, which provided recommendations and mapped processes (ESU, 2012). These guidelines and operational manuals are part of the governmental techniques that convey a neoliberal form of government and educate people without becoming responsible for them. Besides defining criteria to sanction wrongdoings, definitions and penalties, guidelines also encourage employers in New Zealand to contact the ESU to check workers' status and report 'unacceptable' behaviour. The varying interpretations of these guidelines and manuals and the limited reach of the New Zealand Labour inspectors are the backdrop for their operationalisation.

Before banning workers from the scheme, team leaders first label them as troublemakers. On top of the constant reminders to behave accordingly, if someone 'gets into trouble', leaders can prevent workers from going outside their lodges during their free time. Sanctioned workers comply with restrictions and remain indoors, often being told again the same behavioural rules. In some cases, unsubstantiated banning occurs based on rumours of extra-marital relations, drinking, etc. Individuals can be publicly named and shamed, or called aside to be reprimanded. To avoid this, workers can remain silent about grievances in order to avoid being labelled as troublemakers. This singling out contributes to public shame, which can be incapacitating. In Vanuatu, and generally across Pacific countries, respect to elders and community leaders is the norm, and individuals are expected to respect culture and traditions and not to shame their family.[23]

---

[22] New Zealand's Crimes Act of 1961, the Wages Protection Act of 1983, and the Immigration Act have only led to human trafficking convictions in 2016 and 2020.

[23] Under COVID, these cultural norms were used to prevent absconding in Australia (Petrou, Connell, 2023a).

Team leaders do not take banning lightly and avoid recommending their employers not to retain a worker, due to retaliation concerns against fellow co-nationals. New Zealand media coverage of these incidents also supports the disciplining of workers, rarely providing voice to RSE workers but to employers or industry representatives (Enoka, 2019). The high number of applicants facilitates this form of disciplining, as non-retuning workers can easily be replaced. Leaders and workers deal with prohibitions differently. During fieldwork, silences when discussing banning were common and consistent around potentially problematic or contested matters. The link between these silences and workers not wanting to undermine their participation in the scheme, became clearer after several interview rounds. Workers were protecting their interests and so, by implication, could not contest sanctioning decisions, even though they may have been unfounded, based on rumours and/or prejudice. Affecting their families and communities, not only through the lack of remittances from the current agricultural season, but also because being unable to participate in following seasons can stigmatise individuals, hinder their ability to work, and improve their financial situation and that of their families in the long run. Additionally, relatives' knowledge of the reasons for workers not returning has implications for their social standing.

4.6 Being on the Safe Side? Safety and Security Matters

Safety and security concerns are addressed to retain workers' productivity. Team leaders take preventative measures restricting access to bars, advising workers not to walk around alone, forbidding sports, or monitoring alcohol use. Security from local criminal activity in the areas where workers live, entails protecting foreign workers from petty crime, as they are considered easy prey for being sold counterfeit merchandise, drugs, or becoming victims of scams. Restrictions often placed on workers' movements[24] over safety concerns are gendered. Women and men have separate accommodations to prevent sexual health related incidents and are subject to different oversight. Some ni-Vanuatu perceive the outside as threatening due to corrupting forces, thus preventing potential crimes by staying indoors and avoiding walking around (Eriksen, 2016) is acceptable.

Cultural differences and the presence of young people are reasons for prohibitions, particularly for women (Cummings, 2013b) and are often conveyed in the interest of their safety. Workers' team leaders, relatives in New Zealand, and co-workers, can monitor women's behaviour. Team leaders encouraged: 'that ladies don't walk around by themselves, they have to be accompanied by two

---

[24] See Petrou and Connell (2023a) for mobility restrictions in the SWP.

men while walking on the streets [...] We always remind them [...] and when it comes to the time that someone breaks it and get into problems, I said you go home. I tell them is not new to you, so don't come and cry to me' (oral communication, Harry, team leader, Hawke's Bay, 31-05-2014). Contesting such arrangements is difficult, and some women, considered they were treated 'just like children' because of their free time restrictions. Often the boundaries for good behaviour were unclear and women felt they were subject to many rules not applied to men. This made them cautious about new friendships and relating to others outside the group they were living with, partly to prevent gossip and partly due to cultural differences with workers from other nationalities. The construction of risks and how to prevent them is transformed across social relations, through which threats, fears, and worries are shared. Similar concerns from other Pacific countries workers have surfaced in the last years (NZHRC, 2022; Wall, 2020), as it is not only the hierarchies of the scheme, but also the relations from back home that reach from the villages in the form of advice, warnings, or prohibitions.

Difficulties are exacerbated when workers are unable to argue against leaders' decisions, which sometimes may be arbitrary or lack enough basis. A female worker banned from participating in the scheme had no opportunity to contest the rumours of her alleged infidelity, and team leaders used her dismissal to set an example. This has similarities with how 'deportability' (De Genova, Peutz, 2010) operates in the SAWP (Basok, Bélanger, 2016), the model programme for the RSE scheme, and whereby migrants live under the pressure of a potential deportation, some of them being deported so others can remain as workers. Workers on these type of employer-assisted temporary work visas become vulnerable due to their employer dependency to maintain their visa status. This situation creates pressure to perform to the employer's satisfaction to prevent dismissal, because if their contract is rescinded workers can no longer legally remain in the country and thus become at risk of being deported (Binford, 2009). The penalisation of romantic affairs is problematic. Workers have to 'commit not to engage in romantic relationships' by signing a Code of Conduct (ESU, 2019). This curtailment of freedoms is also questionable from a Western standpoint, where personal decisions such as having romantic relationships are private and not subject to supervisors' disciplinary action. By extension employers' support of team leaders' decisions, evidence the consequences of making third parties responsible for the prevention of potential problems such as absconding and sexual health related risks.[25]

---

[25] These concerns are defended because workers' insurance does not cover pregnancy expenses. Before COVID, women were repatriated in case of pregnancy (Bailey, Bedford, 2020), but travel restrictions made this impossible during border closures.

Alcohol consumption is strongly governed through formal and informal means.[26] The abovementioned Code of Conduct signed before embarking on a trip, prohibits alcohol consumption in relation to causing problems at work or in public places (ESU, 2019). The 'alcohol-free brand' was used since 2011 as a marketing strategy to promote the hiring of ni-Vanuatu over workers from other nationalities (ESU, 2014). These rules were generally enforced by employers, some having a legally questionable zero-tolerance alcohol policy on their premises and the lodges they rent. Police officers cannot legally enforce alcohol bans, or other restrictions imposed by the government of Vanuatu, as the RSE scheme bilateral agreements only allow decisions consistent with existing laws and policies in the receiving country (Luthria, Malaulau, 2013). Additionally, the current New Zealand Health and Safety Act (2015) does not prohibit alcohol consumption for similar occupations, apart from during working shifts or in indoor workplaces. This prohibition is not about reducing workplace injuries, as hazard management should be carried out by law, but to avoid potential incidents after working hours.

As employers are responsible for lodging workers, they have the prerogative to regulate, at their own discretion, workers' activities while on their private property and during non-working hours. Some of the lodges where workers stay have cameras operating 24/7. Alcohol-related incidents connected to criminal offences such as damage to property or drunk driving, though sporadic, gained media attention during the first years of the scheme and later under COVID (Bedford, Bailey, 2022). These incidents are usually managed by sending workers home. Among workers, alcohol consumption is frequently debated, though not exempt from ambivalence: 'But only we, us here in this lots [company] we follow the rules that [they] tell us. But all the other companies not [...] that's not fair [...] on the other [hand] is good, when you are here you spend money. So, it's good that you are not drinking here, you can save your money, [your] allowance' (oral communication, Geoffrey, 4th RSE season, Hawke's Bay, 31-05-2014).

Workers and government officers alike made vague mentions of deportation during my fieldwork. For example, drinking and inebriation are not crimes or sufficient cause for deportation under New Zealand law. However, some workers understood colleagues had been deported for alcohol-related problems: 'You drank and they fine you, they only fine you one time, [the company] give[s] you [a] chance, number two, no more chance, you go [to] prison. [RSE employers say to] somebodys you must no work more, you go to prison, come back [to Vanuatu] ...

---

[26] Strict alcohol bans are institutionalised for Samoa, Tonga, and Vanuatu. In Samoa, village councils require returned RSE workers not to consume alcohol as a condition for their return to New Zealand. Some villages consider this a positive change (Bedford, C., Bedford, R. & Nunns, 2020).

strict, strict' (oral communication, Nako, 3rd RSE season, Hawke's Bay, 31-05-2014). In a context where alcohol bans in public places can lead to prosecutions and have increasingly led to criminalisation (Binford, 2009; Webb, Marriott-Lloyd & Grenfell, 2004), already disadvantaged groups can be further stigmatised.

Some leaders have carte blanche to establish standards in the living quarters workers share inside or outside employers' premises. In one of the lodges visited, the leader had banned television use after 9 pm and vetted the programmes watched; others had curfews. None of the few accommodations I visited in 2015 had Internet access and very few workers then had a smartphone. Connectivity was still an issue in 2020 (Bedford, C., Bedford, R. & Nunns, 2020). A pastoral care worker argued companies do not connect lodges to the Internet because this could lead to watching pornography, thus preventing liability and opening the door for other problems. Leaders can also prohibit workers from playing sports to avoid injuries which would affect their productivity and earnings. Tensions between respecting workers' private life and basic civil liberties, in order to keeping workers productive are commonplace.

In Vanuatu, letters of endorsement from village chiefs, church leaders and/or spouses are a requirement to apply for the RSE scheme limited visa. Married applicants request letters from their spouses, while younger applicants, may ask their parents. 'Good character' reference letters from local authorities vouch for the applicant's behaviour, indicate mutual agreement with the trip and sometimes include obligations in the community after return. '[Pastors] have to know that you are very good, [that you had a Christian] conversion, [that] you are humble, that you are ok. [...] the chief has also to make a reference in order that you are good recommended. You couldn't have a bad background' (oral communication, Tim, former RSE team leader, Santo, 26-10-2014). These letters are neither part of the official RSE scheme documentation nor required by the New Zealand government to process visa applications, but accepting this practice legitimises these means to discipline workers. Religious male-dominated hierarchy and sex-segregated roles also ensure conformity with established norms. Besides church officials assisting workers' selection, they collaborate during workers' absence ensuring families are looked-after and can also make requirements of returnees, such as financial contributions or commitments to support church initiatives (Bailey, 2013; Maclellan, 2008). Non-traditional churches, which are usually break-away churches that separated from Anglican or Presbyterian denominations, integrate Vanuatu customary values to a certain extent, into their Christian doctrine. In the same way, individualistic values can blend in with 'Pentecostalisation' processes, creating new ways of living and thinking (Rio, Eriksen, 2014; Rio, 2019).

Because migration is considered to have the potential of creating crises, accepting this additional layer of third-parties' management could avoid government liability, creating the impression that private individuals retain control. Having pre-arranged accommodation provided by employers, workers cannot legally be allowed to live elsewhere. Working where they live and living where they work have many implications. Some employers do not allow married couples to sleep together or share a bedroom, or prohibit single workers to be visited by partners or outsiders to the lodging facilities. Regulations as discipline techniques transfer the responsibility for the conduct of workers to private actors, namely team leaders, employers, pastoral care agents, or community members; seemingly in response to a cost–benefit calculation by state actors. They have the advantage of having expertise and resources on the ground. In intervening more closely, public–private boundaries are redrawn and authority shifts towards new actors (Kunz, 2008). Nonetheless, the operation of these techniques depends on who articulates them, and on how information flows through social relations in a dynamic process that intertwines customary and neoliberal values.

4.7 Something Ventured, Something Lost?

For development to be realised, workers sign a contract to be on good behaviour and become compliant to both official and unofficial rules operationalised in the management of the scheme. Ni-Vanuatu cultural values of respect, humility and their communal approach, makes them ideal workers as it is hard for them to complain or stand up to their employers. Compliance and discipline extend beyond working hours, work grounds, and overlap with workers' leisure time as living on their employer's premises they have to behave as if they were at work after working hours. The prohibitions on drinking during their free time, on cohabitating with their partners or spouses, and not being allowed to maintain intimate relations in the housing facilities rented by them, are highly problematic and conflict with basic civil and individual liberties (NZHRC, 2022; Wall, 2020).

When individuals are made responsible for the life in their communities, they meet discipline with consent, whether consciously or unconsciously. Conscious consent implies the exercise of self-care by adhering to behavioural rules that are at once prescriptions and truths. Self-care interacts with direct forms of discipline, making workers compliant while expecting to be rewarded with continued employment. At times the 'good behaviour' is controlled by team leaders, colleagues, employers, or their own families. The knowledge of what makes a good worker defines behavioural boundaries. Formal instances such as trainings, and informal practices in daily interactions with leaders and among workers communicate expectations. By observing, monitoring and disciplining workers using the development idiom, compliant subjects are formed. But becoming a RSE worker extends personal responsibility to collective behaviour, so workers are consciously careful not to jeopardise others' chances to continue in the scheme.

Workers compensate for their absence by becoming good providers, kinsmen, and community members. There is also a sense of achievement, satisfaction, and pride when material goals are fulfilled and individuals are able to take care of their own expenses, such as when paying for customary weddings without incurring in debt or owing favours to relatives. This situates individuals in different positions, potentially granting them a different social status. It was unclear whether not having a debt usually incurred through a customary wedding, could signal distancing from existing social relations or a change in enduring exchange relations. Changes in housing materials and housing dispersion also seem to be contributing to distancing RSE scheme participants from community work and community life in a wider sense (Smith, 2018; Smith, 2021). The new wealth obtained may also create tensions within villages (Craven, 2015; Smith, 2016), leading to the questioning of traditional communal practices (Bedford, C., Bedford, R. & Nunns, 2020). To justify their new status and attitudes, returnees often refer to the efforts and sacrifices endured in New Zealand, which in their opinion can relieve them from communal labour contributions and other responsibilities they would have carried out before their departure.

During my fieldwork years, workers' perceptions and attitudes towards their continuation in the scheme changed. Ambivalence and complicity were part and parcel of workers' lives in New Zealand. Secrets were kept regarding what workers did in their private time, some leaders allowed more freedom on the condition matters were kept from anyone's knowledge. Some workers were planning to disengage from the scheme once their goals had been fulfilled, while others set a time horizon. However, plans changed, sometimes encouraged by team leaders, because their employer had included workers' name on the return list, or by new economic and material needs of their families. Intentions to disengage seem related to workers' age, the strength they felt, and are also conditional on becoming financially independent after fulfilling some material goals at home or creating new businesses to buy their way out of the scheme. Workers have also increasingly become more vocal, some of them questioning the extent of their engagement in the RSE scheme (Bailey, 2014; Stead & Petrou, 2023), and Pacific governments have become more assertive since COVID began.

5 Conclusions

The RSE scheme is symptomatic of the accepted development model for Pacific countries and their purported transition from semi-subsistence economies to neoliberal states. The problematisation of being young, poor and unemployed was constructed as a predicament of individuals, made responsible to improve their own situation. The coupling of these demographics with the lack of labour in New Zealand at peak times of the agricultural season, made temporary migration an agreeable solution. Despite aiming for a replication of migration management good practices, assumptions and biases are notorious in the operationalisation of the scheme due to its epistemic and political underpinnings. Relying not only on migrants' responsibilities, but also on the articulation of a network of actors and stakeholders the scheme is driven by a development narrative. To make issues manageable, this narrative oversimplifies the complexity of issues at hand, risking at the same time essentialising workers through comparisons of measurable differences on economic indicators.

Without the coupling of migration and development, the RSE scheme would arguably not be able to function, as the assumptions of mutual benefits among its stakeholders justifies its continuation. The narratives of cost-benefit economic assessments and the aggregates of economy wide benefits largely used to monitor and evaluate migration programmes, discount migration less tangible effects in the lives of migrants. By bringing attention to political dimensions at different analytical scales, from regional to individual perspectives, the governmentality framework allowed for the possibility of understanding relations between RSE scheme participants and policy-makers in a dynamic way over time and space. In systematically assessing the knowledge claims that inform migration management regulations, incentives, and development interventions, the historical context underpinning policy-making was brought to the fore.

There are interesting parallels between the material transformations of the late Nineteenth century with those underway today. Not only cultural aspects are being transformed with the construction of new housing and the consumer goods purchased; remuneration, work experiences, and material encounters also transform meaningful social relations. These transformations entail a network of new social obligations mediated by money and objects and are telling of the power relations in which they are enmeshed, as a continuation of long-standing global forces that have shaped workers' engagement with the more developed economies in the region. While it is possible to identify some salient changes, social transformation depends on multiple factors and it is not simply the result of individuals' participation in the RSE scheme, but of the interaction with local worldviews and the amplification of social and material networks among migrant workers, as well as among government officials from Pacific countries who are expected to learn from their more developed neighbours, reinforcing notions of aid through government officers and employers' narratives. Just as it is difficult for Pacific countries to contest the development narratives, under the same logic, compliance with the requirements to 'win' under the scheme often remain uncontested by workers.

The RSE scheme is something migrants are shaping through their own choices and actions as they engage in a space of regulated freedom prescribed by the boundaries of their limited working visa. Labour mobility provides Pacific people with the economic right to work in a developed economy and to earn a living. Nonetheless, the trade-offs of this engagement, such as the unduly household dependence on this income (Bedford, C., Bedford, R. & Nunns, 2020) and existing restrictions, pose the question whether the right to work that Pacific people gain is itself dependent on not enjoying other fundamental rights and guarantees in the destination country, or on their use of culturally intelligible strategies to deal with the prospect of becoming return workers. Negotiation of workers' social, political, and economic positions with themselves and with the managers of labour mobility are the backdrop of their participation in the scheme. Departures can be calculated decisions, but are also emotional ones, and new forms of subjectivation can lead to significant social, productive and reproductive transformation. The acquisition of status, the remittances, goods, and property obtained with migrants' earnings transform participants' communities as new statuses, roles, relations and positions emerge. Individuals can gauge their own self-worth and compare themselves among the winners and the losers – in label and experience – within a scheme that aims to produce just winners.

This research's insights regarding the transformation of ni-Vanuatu subjectivities relate mostly to the personal and social consequences for individuals, families, communities, and sending countries. In the idiom of labour mobility and through the development narratives, individuals have become RSE workers. This highlights what individuals do, rather than where they live, where they come from, or who they are. Personal characteristics such as physical prowess and the emotional strength needed to be away from their families, are conditions that workers have internalised they need to succeed in the scheme. They justify learning to cope with the distance and the requirements of work and off-work hours, because their earnings will eventually procure their children's education or allow them to become financially independent. Being away from home is especially hard for the few women participants. Their decision to migrate and their childcare arrangements are changing some social practices and familial responsibilities when friends, village chiefs, extended families, or religious groups step in to look after family members while workers are away for months. Many migrants from the Global South face similar transformations when they delegate their own productive and reproductive roles to others.

The empowering and disempowering character of these transformations justify these changes as a means to achieve what the RSE idiom promotes as development, but these changes also become an end in themselves. This speaks about how through development narratives, social issues that may not be considered problematic in societies that are not fully capitalistic, are problematised when viewed from elsewhere. For example, considering the cultural diversity of Pacific countries as an asset rather than a communications obstacle for Westerners, can help widen other perspectives, given that economic development is only one way of understanding reality. Solutions to constructed development problems intentionally transmit a set of values for subjects to become more easily incorporated to global economic processes. Development, thus encompasses sets of social practices adopted through the operation of governmental techniques, as it is only through participants' transformations that they become productive subjects. New social relations – such as the one between an employer and an employee – engender new subjectivities entangled in neoliberal values, which sometimes conflict with more traditional customary values, and other times capitalise on them.

Research on migration from a governmentality perspective in the Pacific region is nascent. Future research on temporary migration should incorporate political dimensions to the existing economic ones to provide fuller interpretations of complex and shifting relationships, and examine places through the transformation of migrants' subjectivities, for example, from a postcolonial or post-development standpoint. Drawing attention to the historical context of mobility in the Pacific, the social transformations in migrants' communities, and the new configurations in their social relations, which support a repetitive pattern of absence for significant periods of time, can have far reaching implications. Relational analyses can unveil the materiality of workers' experiences, their meaningful social relations, and their limited bargaining power due to existing power differentials. Unveiling the relations underpinning shared knowledge can also contribute to new insights regarding the challenges that particular groups of people face, based on how they transform their own behaviours when their agency is curtailed by the conditions of their limited work visa.

This research's contribution resonates with the increasing interest in the region, to know more about the hidden costs of labour mobility and the long-term implications of temporary migration. Understanding new processes of subjectivation, can also suggest future directions for development practice, particularly, at a time when Pacific countries are reconsidering the type of development they want post-COVID and questioning whether earning a living through labour mobility is preferable to revitalising their own economies.

References

Adamson, F. B. & Tsourapas, G. 2020, "The migration state in the global south: Nationalizing, developmental, and neoliberal models of migration management", *International Migration Review*, vol. 54, no. 3, pp. 853–882.

Andrijasevic, R. & Walters, W. 2010, "The international organization for migration and the international government of borders", *Environment and Planning D: Society and Space*, vol. 28, no. 6, pp. 977–999.

Astonitas, L. M. 2018, *Seasons of change: Ni-Vanuatu and the Recognised Seasonal Employer's (RSE) scheme*, PhD. thesis, Waipapa Taumata Rau University of Auckland.

AusAID. 2006, *Pacific 2020: Challenges and opportunities for growth*, AusAID Australian Agency for International Development, Canberra.

Badkar, J. U., Callister, P. & Didham, R. A. 2009, *Ageing New Zealand: The growing reliance on migrant caregivers*, Institute of Policy Studies, Washington, DC.

Bailey, R. 2017, *The Role of ni-Vanuatu Team Leaders in Seasonal Worker Programs*, State, Society & Governance in Melanesia Australian National University, Canberra.

Bailey, R. 2014, *Working the Vines: Seasonal migration, money, and development in New Zealand and Ambrym, Vanuatu*, PhD. thesis, University of Otago.

Bailey, R. 2013, *Ni-Vanuatu in the Recognised Seasonal Employer Scheme: Impacts at home and away*, SSGM Discussion Paper 2013/4. Australian National University, Canberra.

Bailey, R. & Bedford, C. 2020, *COVID-19: RSE responses, challenges and logistics*, Crawford School of Public Policy, Australian National University.

Bailey, R., Bumseng, P. & Bumseng, R. 2016, *Labour Mobility Support Networks – 'It's Not Just a Seasonal Thing'*, SSGM IB2016/23. Australian National University, Canberra.

Barker, F. 2010, "Maximizing the migration policy buck: Uniting temporary labor, development and foreign policy goals in New Zealand", *Policy and Society*, vol. 29, no. 4, pp. 321–331.

Bartels, I. 2017, "'We must do it gently.' The contested implementation of the IOM's migration management in Morocco", *Migration Studies*, vol. 5, no. 3, pp. 315–336.

Basok, T. 2002, *Tortillas and tomatoes: Transmigrant Mexican harvesters in Canada*, McGill-Queen's University Press, Montreal.

References

Basok, T. & Bélanger, D. 2016, "Migration management, disciplinary power, and performances of subjectivity: Agricultural migrant workers' in Ontario", *Canadian Journal of Sociology*, vol. 41, no. 2, pp. 139–163.

Basok, T., Piper, N. & Simmons, V. 2013, "Disciplining female migration in Argentina: Human rights in the time of migration management" in *Disciplining the Transnational Mobility of People*, eds. M. Geiger & A. Pécoud, Palgrave Macmillan, Basingstoke; New York, pp. 162–184.

Bedford, C. 2013, *Picking winners?: New Zealand's Recognised Seasonal Employer (RSE) policy and its impacts on employers, Pacific workers and their island-based communities*, Ph.D. thesis, University of Adelaide.

Bedford, C. & Bailey, R. 2022, *Managing Worker Wellbeing during COVID-19: Pacific Seasonal Workers in Australia and New Zealand*, Working Paper 2021/1, Department of Pacific Affairs, Australian National University.

Bedford, C., Bedford, R. & Ho, E. 2010, "Engaging with New Zealand's recognized seasonal employer work policy: The case of Tuvalu", *Asian and Pacific Migration Journal*, vol. 19, no. 3, pp. 412–445.

Bedford, C., Bedford, R. & Nunns, H. 2020, *RSE Impact Study: Pacific stream report*, Ministry of Business Innovation and Employment (MBIE), Wellington.

Bedford, R. 2008, "Pasifika mobility: Pathways, circuits, and challenges in the 21st century" in *Pacific interactions* in *Pasifika in New Zealand, New Zealand in Pasifika*, ed. A. Bisley, Institute of Policy Studies, School of Government, Victoria University of Wellington, Wellington, pp. 85–134.

Bedford, R. 2006, "Trends in Pacific demography: Push and pull factors for labour supply" in *The future of the Pacific labour market: Labour mobility in the Pacific*, ed. N. Plimmer, Pacific Cooperation Foundation, Wellington, pp. 45–52.

Bedford, R. 1973, *New Hebridean mobility: A study of circular migration*, Australian National University, Canberra.

Bedford, R., & Bedford, C. 2023, "How many seasonal workers from the Pacific have been employed in New Zealand since the RSE scheme began?" *New Zealand Geographer*, vol. 79, no. 1, pp. 39–45.

Bedford, R., Bedford, C., Wall, J. & Young, M. 2017, "Managed temporary labour migration of Pacific Islanders to Australia and New Zealand in the early twenty-first century", *Australian Geographer*, vol. 48, no. 1, pp. 37–57.

Bedford, R. & Hugo, G. 2008, *International migration in a sea of islands: Challenges and opportunities for insular Pacific spaces*, Population Studies Centre, University of Waikato, Hamilton.

References

Binford, L. 2009, "From fields of power to fields of sweat: The dual process of constructing temporary migrant labour in Mexico and Canada", *Third World Quarterly*, vol. 30, no. 3, pp. 503–517.

Boltanski, L. & Chiapello, E. 2005, "The new spirit of capitalism", *International Journal of Politics, Culture, and Society*, vol. 18, no. 3, pp. 161–188.

Booth, A. 1994, *Employment, unemployment and access of education: Policy dilemmas for a poor Pacific economy*, Dept. of Economics, School of Oriental and African Studies, University of London, London.

Borovnik, M. 2011, "Occupational health and safety of merchant seafarers from Kiribati and Tuvalu", *Asia Pacific Viewpoint*, vol. 52, no. 3, pp. 333–346.

Borovnik, M. 2009, "Transnationalism of merchant seafarers and their communities in Kiribati and Tuvalu" in *Pacific transnationalism*, eds. H. Lee & S. Francis, ANU Press, Canberra, pp. 143–157.

Borovnik, M. 2005, "Seafarers 'maritime culture' and the I-Kiribati way of life: The formation of flexible identities?", *Singapore Journal of Tropical Geography*, vol. 26, no. 2, pp. 132–150.

Brinkerhoff, J. 2008, "Diasporas and development What Role for Foreign Aid?" in *Foreign aid and foreign policy: Lessons for the next half-century*, eds. L. A. Picard, R. Groelsema & T.F. Buss, Armonk, London, pp. 375–393.

Carens, J. H. 2008, "Live-in domestics, seasonal workers, and others hard to locate on the map of democracy", *Journal of Political Philosophy*, vol. 16, no. 4, pp. 419–445.

Carrete, J. & King, R. 2005, *Selling spirituality the silent takeover of religion*, Routledge, London; New York.

Chapman, M. 1986, "Me go 'walkabout', you too?" in *Circulation in population movement: Substance and concepts from the Melanesian case*, eds. M. Chapman & R. M. Prothero, reprinted ed., East-West Center, Honolulu, pp. 429–442.

Chapman, M. & Prothero, M. 1986, "Circulation between 'home' and other places: Some propositions" in *Circulation in population movement: Substance and concepts from the Melanesian case*, eds. M. Chapman & R. M. Prothero, reprinted ed., East-West Center, Honolulu, pp. 1–12.

Clear Horizon. 2016, *SPP and Vakameasina Evaluation Report*, Ministry of Foreign Affairs and Trade, Wellington.

Clough, P. T. 2010, "The case of sociology: Governmentality and methodology", *Critical Inquiry*, vol. 36, no. 4, pp. 627–641.

Collins, F. L. 2021, "Temporary migration and regional development amidst Covid-19: Invercargill and Queenstown", *New Zealand Geographer*, vol. 77, no. 3, pp. 191–205.

Collins, F. L. 2020, "Legislated inequality: Provisional migration and the stratification of migrant lives" in *Intersections of inequality, migration and diversification*, eds. R. Simon-Kumar, F.L. Collins & W. Friesen, Palgrave Pivot, Cham, pp. 65–86.

Connell, J. 2015, "Temporary labour migration in the Pacific" in *Migration and development: Perspectives from small states*, ed. W.H. Khonje, Commonwealth Secretariat, London, pp. 60–91.

Connell, J. 2010, "Pacific islands in the global economy: Paradoxes of migration and culture", *Singapore Journal of Tropical Geography*, vol. 31, no. 1, pp. 115–129.

Connell, J. 1984, "Islands under pressure: Population growth and urbanization in the South Pacific", *Ambio*, vol. 13, no. 5, pp. 306–312.

Connell, J. & Lee, H. 2018, *Change and continuity in the Pacific: Revisiting the region*, Routledge, Oxon.

Connell, J. & Walton-Roberts, M. 2016, "What about the workers? The missing geographies of health care", *Progress in Human Geography*, vol. 40, no. 2, pp. 158–176.

Coppedge, S. 2006, *People trafficking an international crisis fought at the local level*, Fulbright New Zealand.

Courtney, C. 2008, *Growing Pains*, North & South, 2008, no. 265, pp. 70–79, Bauer Media Group.

Craven, L. 2015, "Migration-affected change and vulnerability in rural Vanuatu", *Asia Pacific Viewpoint*, vol. 56, no. 2, pp. 223–236.

Cummings, M. 2013a, "Imagining transnational futures in Vanuatu" in *A companion to diaspora and transnationalism*, eds. A. Quayson & G. Daswani, Blackwell, Oxford, pp. 381–396.

Cummings, M. 2013b, "Looking good: The cultural politics of the island dress for young women in Vanuatu", *The Contemporary Pacific*, vol. 25, no. 1, pp. 33–65.

Curtain, R., Dornan, M., Doyle, J. & Howes, S. 2016, *Labour mobility: The ten billion dollar prize*, World Bank, Washington, DC.

Curtain, R., Dornan, M., Howes, S. & Sherrell, H. 2018, "Pacific seasonal workers: Learning from the contrasting temporary migration outcomes in Australian and New Zealand horticulture", *Asia & the Pacific Policy Studies*, vol. 5, no. 3, pp. 462–480.

De Genova, N. 2009, "Conflicts of mobility, and the mobility of conflict: Rightlessness, presence, subjectivity, freedom", *Subjectivity*, vol. 29, no. 1, pp. 445–466.

De Genova, N. 2006, "The legal production of Mexican/migrant 'Illegality'" in *Latinos and citizenship: The dilemma of belonging*, ed. S. Oboler, Palgrave Macmillan, New York, pp. 61–90.

References

De Genova, N. 2002, "Migrant 'illegality' and deportability in everyday life", *Annual Review of Anthropology*, vol. 31, no. 1, pp. 419–447.

De Genova, N. & Peutz, N. M. 2010, *The deportation regime: Sovereignty, space, and the freedom of movement*, Duke University Press, Durham.

de Vries, P. 2007, "Don't compromise your desire for development! A Lacanian/Deleuzian rethinking of the anti-politics machine", *Third World Quarterly*, vol. 28, no. 1, pp. 25–43.

Dean, M. 1999, *Governmentality: Power and rule in modern society*, Sage, London, Thousand Oaks.

Dibb, P., Hale, D. & Prince, P. 1999, "Asia's insecurity", *Survival*, vol. 41, no. 3, pp. 5–20.

Dobell, G. 2012, "From 'arc of instability' to 'arc of responsibility'", *Security Challenges*, vol. 8, no. 4, pp. 33–45.

Duffield, M. 2006, "Racism, migration and development: The foundations of planetary order", *Progress in Development Studies*, vol. 6, no. 1, pp. 68–79.

Duffield, M. 2001, *Global governance and the new wars: The merging of development and security*, Zed Books; Palgrave, London; New York.

Dun, O., Klocker, N., Farbotko, C. & McMichael, C. 2023, "Climate change adaptation in agriculture: Learning from an international labour mobility programme in Australia and the Pacific Islands region", *Environmental Science & Policy*, vol. 139, pp. 250–273.

Duncan, R. & Chand, S. 2002, "The economics of the 'arc of instability'", *Asian-Pacific Economic Literature*, vol. 16, no. 1, pp. 1–9.

Duncan, R. 2008, "Cultural and economic tensions in Pacific Islands' futures", *International Journal of Social Economics*, vol. 35, no. 12, pp. 919–929.

Enoka, A. J. 2019, *Under the gaze: A study of the portrayal by the New Zealand print media of Pacific Island workers in the Recognised Seasonal Employer (RSE) scheme, 2007–2012*, Ph.D. thesis, Massey University.

Eriksen, A. 2016, "The virtuous woman and the holy nation: Femininity in the context of Pentecostal Christianity in Vanuatu", *The Australian Journal of Anthropology*, vol. 27, no. 2, pp. 260–275.

Eriksen, A. 2009, "'New life': Pentecostalism as social critique in Vanuatu", *Ethnos*, vol. 74, no. 2, pp. 175–198.

ESU. 2019, *Information guide for agents recruiting workers for the Recognised Seasonal Employer (RSE) and Seasonal Worker Program (SWP)*, Vanuatu Department of Labour, Port Vila.

ESU. 2014, *Work ready Vanuatu presentation*, Vanuatu Department of Labour, Port Vila.

References

ESU. 2013, *Stand down and ban policy information guide*, Vanuatu Department of Labour, Port Vila. www.workreadyvanuatu.com/documents/ [25.05.2014].

ESU. 2012, *Process overview map of RSE and SWP*. Vanuatu Department of Labour, Port Vila.

Faist, T. 2008, "Migrants as transnational development agents: An inquiry into the newest round of the migration–development nexus", *Population, Space and Place*, vol. 14, no. 1, pp. 21–42.

Faist, T., Fauser, M. & Kivisto, P. 2011, *The migration-development nexus a transnational perspective*, Palgrave Macmillan, Houndmills, Baskingstoke, Hampshire; New York.

Foucault, M. 2008, *The birth of biopolitics: Lectures at the Collège de France, 1978–79*, Palgrave Macmillan, Houndmills, Basingstoke, Hampshire England; New York.

Foucault, M. 2007, *Security, territory, population: Lectures at the Collège de France, 1977–78*, Palgrave Macmillan, Basingstoke; New York.

Foucault, M. 2003, *Society must be defended: Lectures at the Collège de France, 1975–76*, Penguin, London.

Foucault, M. 2001, "Governmentality" in *Power. Vol. 3 of The Essential Works of Foucault, 1954–1984*, ed. J. D. Faubion. Trans. Robert Hurley et al. Penguin, London, pp. 201–222.

Foucault, M. 1991, "Questions of method" in *The Foucault effect: Studies in governmentality with two lectures and an interview by Michel Foucault*, eds. G. Burchell, C. Gordon & P. Miller, University of Chicago Press, Chicago, pp. 73–86.

Foucault, M. 1980, "Truth and power" in, ed. C. Gordon, Harvester Wheatsheaf, New York; London; Toronto; Sydney; Tokyo; Singapore, pp. 109–133.

Friesen, W. 2018, "Beyond the RSE: Systems of Pacific labour migration to New Zealand", *New Zealand Population Review*, vol. 44, pp. 111–129.

GCIM. 2005, *Migration in an interconnected world, new directions for action*, Global Commission on International Migration, Geneva.

Geiger, M. 2013, "The transformation of migration politics: From migration control to disciplining mobility" in *Disciplining the transnational mobility of people*, eds. M. Geiger & A. Pécoud, Palgrave Macmillan, Houndmills; Basingstoke; Hampshire, pp. 15–40.

Geiger, M. & Pécoud, A. 2010, *The politics of international migration management*, Palgrave Macmillan, Basingstoke; Hampshire; New York.

Georgi, F. 2010, "For the benefit of some: The international organization for migration and its global migration management" in *The politics of international migration management*, eds. M. Geiger & A. Pécoud, Springer, Basingstoke; New York, pp. 45–72.

Ghosh, B. 2000, "Towards a new international regime for orderly movements of people" in *Managing migration: Time for a new international regime?* ed. B. Ghosh, Oxford University Press, Oxford, pp. 6–26.

Gibson, J. & Bailey, R. 2021, "Seasonal labor mobility in the Pacific: Past impacts, future prospects", *Asian Development Review*, vol. 38, no. 1, pp. 1–32.

Hau'ofa, E. 1994, "Our sea of islands", *The Contemporary Pacific*, vol. 6, no. 1, pp. 147–161.

Hayes, G. 2010, *Maximizing development benefits and minimizing negative impact of international migration in the Pacific Islands sub-region*, UNESCAP, Workshop on Strengthening National Capacities to Deal with International Migration, 22–23 April, Bangkok.

Hess, S. 2009, *Person and place: Ideas, ideals and practice of sociality on Vanua Lava, Vanuatu*, Berghahn Books, New York.

Hoadley, S. 2005, *Pacific island security management by New Zealand & Australia: Towards a new paradigm*, Centre for Strategic Studies New Zealand, Wellington.

Hugo, G. 2009, "Care worker migration, Australia and development", *Population, Space and Place*, vol. 15, no. 2, pp. 189–203.

Hugo, G. & Bedford, R. 2017, "Migration agreements and regional integration in the Pacific" in *Migration, free movement and regional integration*, eds. S. Nita, A. Pécoud, P. de Lombaerde, K. Neyts & J. Gartland, UNESCO, Paris, pp. 395–425.

ILO. 2015, "The Recognized Seasonal Employers scheme (RSE), New Zealand", *MIGRANT Labor Migration Brand, Good Practices Database – Labour Migration Policies and Programmes*. Geneva.

IMSED Research. 2010, *Final Evaluation Report of the Recognised Seasonal Employer Policy (2007–2009)*, Department of Labour, Wellington.

INZ. 2010, *Operational Manual: WH1 Recognised Seasonal Employer (RSE) Instructions. WH1.20 Requirements for employment agreements under RSE Instructions. Effective 29/11/2010*, Wellington.

IOM. 2004, *Essentials of migration management – A guide for policy makers and practitioners*, International Organisation for Migration, Geneva.

Iredale, R.R., Voigt-Graf, C. & Khoo, S. 2012, "Winners and losers in the mobility of teachers in the Pacific Region: Issues and policy debates", *Diversities*, vol. 14, no. 1, pp. 77–98.

Jolly, M. 1987, "The forgotten women: A history of migrant labour and gender relations in Vanuatu", *Oceania*, vol. 58, no. 2, pp. 119–139.

Jolly, M. 2012. "Material and immaterial relations: Gender, rank and Christianity in Vanuatu" in *The scope of anthropology: Maurice Godelier's work in context*. Berghahn Books, New York, pp. 110–154.

Kabutaulaka, T. T. 2015, "Re-presenting Melanesia: Ignoble savages and Melanesian alter-natives", *The Contemporary Pacific*, vol. 27, no. 1, pp. 110–145.

Kabutaulaka, T. T. 2005, "Australian foreign policy and the RAMSI intervention in Solomon Islands", *The Contemporary Pacific*, vol. 17, no. 2, pp. 283–308.

Kagan, S. 2016, "'On the ship, you can do anything': The impact of international cruiseship employment for I-Kiribati women", *Pacific Studies*, vol. 36, no. 1, pp. 35–51.

Kalm, S. 2010, "Liberalizing movements? The political rationality of global migration management" in *The politics of international migration management*, eds. M. Geiger & A. Pécoud, Palgrave Macmillan, Basingstoke; Hampshire; New York, pp. 21–44.

Kapur, D. 2004, *Remittances: The new development mantra?* United Nations Conference on Trade and Development, Geneva.

Karal, D. 2018, *Ethico-political governmentality of immigration and asylum: The case of Ethiopia*, Palgrave Macmillan, Cham.

King, R. 2018, Is migration a form of development aid given by poor to rich countries? *Journal of Intercultural Studies*, vol. 39, no. 2, pp. 114–128.

Kunz, R. 2013, "Governing international migration through partnership", *Third World Quarterly*, vol. 34, no. 7, pp. 1227–1246.

Kunz, R. 2008, *Mobilising diasporas: A governmentality analysis of the case of Mexico*, Lucerne.

Larner, W. 1998, "Hitching a ride on the tiger's back: Globalisation and spatial imaginaries in New Zealand", *Environment and Planning D: Society and Space*, vol. 16, no. 5, pp. 599–614.

Lemke, T. 2011, *Biopolitics an advanced introduction*, Project MUSE, 2012 ed., New York University Press, New York.

Lemke, T. 2007, "An indigestible meal? Foucault, governmentality and state theory", *Distinktion: Scandinavian Journal of Social Theory*, vol. 8, no. 2, pp. 43–64.

Lemke, T. 2001, "'The birth of bio-politics': Michel Foucault's lecture at the Collège de France on neo-liberal governmentality", *Economy and Society*, vol. 30, no. 2, pp. 190–207.

Levitt, P. 1998, "Social remittances: Migration driven local-level forms of cultural diffusion", *The International Migration Review*, vol. 32, no. 4, pp. 926–948.

Liangni, S. L., Guanyu, J. R., & Xiaoyun, R. 2022, "New Zealand border restrictions amidst COVID-19 and their impacts on temporary migrant workers", *Asian and Pacific Migration Journal*, vol. 31, no. 3, pp. 1–12.

Libercier, M. H. & Schneider, H. 1996, *Migrants: Partners in development co-operation*, Organisation for Economic Cooperation and Development (OECD), Paris.

Loescher, G. 2001, "The UNHCR and world politics: State interests vs. institutional autonomy", *International Migration Review*, vol. 35, no. 1, pp. 33–56.

Lovelock, K. & Leopold, T. 2008, "Labour force shortages in rural New Zealand: Temporary migration and the Recognised Seasonal Employer (RSE) work policy", *New Zealand Population Review*, vol. 33, no. 34, pp. 213–234.

Luthria, M. & Malaulau, M. 2013, "Bilateral labour agreements in the Pacific: A development" in *Let workers move: Using bilateral labor agreements to increase trade in services*, ed. S. Sáez, The World Bank, Washington, DC, pp. 129–147.

Maclellan, N. 2008, "Seasonal workers for Australia — lessons from New Zealand", *Farm Policy Journal*, vol. 5, no. 3, pp. 43–53.

Maclellan, N. & Mares, P. 2006, "Labour mobility in the Pacific: Creating seasonal work programs in Australia" in *Globalisation and governance in the Pacific Islands. Conference on globalisation and governance in the Pacific Islands*, ed. S. Firth, ANU E Press, Canberra, pp. 137–171.

Māhina-Tuai, K. U. 2012, "FIA (Forgotten in action) Pacific islanders in the New Zealand armed forces" in *Tangata o le moana: New Zealand and the people of the Pacific*, eds. S. Mallon & K.U. Māhina-Tuai, Te Papa Press, Wellington, pp.139–180.

Mark, S. 2022, "New Zealand's public diplomacy in the Pacific: A reset, or more of the same?", *Place Branding and Public Diplomacy*, vol. 18, no. 2, pp. 105–112.

A case study of the governmentalization of the entrepreneur in the French epistemological tradition, *Forum Qualitative Social Research Sozialforschung*, vol. 14, no. 3, pp. 293–331.

May, R. J. 2003, *Arc of instability?: Melanesia in the early 2000s*, State, Society and Governance in Melanesia Project, Research School of Pacific and Asian Studies, Australian National University, Canberra.

McKenzie, D. & Gibson, J. 2014, *Development through seasonal worker programs: The case of New Zealand's RSE Program*, Washington, DC.

McKenzie, D., Garcia Martinez, P. & Winters, L., 2008. *Who is coming from Vanuatu to New Zealand under the new Recognized Seasonal Employer program?* World Bank Policy Research Working Paper 4699, Washington, DC.

Menz, G. 2013, "The neoliberalized state and the growth of the migration industry" in *The migration industry and the commercialization of international migration*, eds. N. Nyberg Sørensen & T. Gammeltoft-Hansen, Routledge, London, pp. 108–127.

Menz, G. 2011, "Neo-liberalism, privatization and the outsourcing of migration management: A five-country comparison", *Competition & Change*, vol. 15, no. 2, pp. 116–135.

MFAT. 2018, *2018 FEMM: Update on Remittances*, Pacific Island Forum Secretariat, Palau.

MFAT. 2007, *Media Pack: Launch of Recognised Seasonal Employer Work Policy*.

Miller, P. & Rose, N. 2008, *Governing the present: Administering economic, social and personal life*, Polity Press, Cambridge; Malden.

Ministry for Primary Industries 2017, *2016 Pipfruit Monitoring Programme*.

Moore, C., Leckie, J. & Munro, D. 1990, *Labour in the South Pacific*, James Cook University of North Queensland, Townsville.

Moore, H. L. 2013, *Still life: Hopes, desires and satisfactions*, 2nd ed., John Wiley, Cambridge; Malden.

Munro, D. 1995, "The labor trade in Melanesians to Queensland: An historiographic essay", *Journal of Social History*, vol. 28, no. 3, pp. 609–627.

Naïr, S. 1997, *Rapport de Bilan et d'Orientation sur la Politique de Codéveloppement Liée aux Flux Migratoires*, Mission Interministérielle 'Migrations/codéveloppement', Paris.

New Zealand Government. 2015, *New Health and Safety at Work Act, New Zealand Legislation*, Public Act.

New Zealand Government. 2014, *Employment Relations Amendment Act 2014, New Zealand Legislation*, Public Act.

New Zealand Government. 2000, *Employment Relations Act 2000 – New Zealand Legislation*, Public Act.

NZHRC. 2022, *The RSE Scheme in Aotearoa New Zealand: A Human Rights Review*, New Zealand Human Rights Commission, Wellington.

Noonan, C. 2011, "Trade negotiations with the Pacific Islands: Promise, process and prognosis", *New Zealand Yearbook of International Law*, vol. 9, pp. 241–283.

Nunns, H., Bedford, C. & Bedford, R. 2019, *RSE impact study: New Zealand stream report*, Ministry of Business Innovation and Employment (MBIE), Wellington.

MBIE. 2015, "The Remittance Pilot Project. The economic benefits of the Recognised Seasonal Employer work policy and its role in assisting development in Samoa and Tonga". MBIE.

Obokata, T. 2010, "Global governance and international migration: A case study of trafficking of human beings", *Refugee Survey Quarterly*, vol. 29, no. 1, pp. 120–136.

OECD. 2014, "Managing labour migration: Smart Policies to support economic growth" in *International migration outlook 2014*, OECD, Paris, pp. 133–232.

OECD. 2011, *Recognised Seasonal Employer (RSE) Worker Pilot Training Programme Vakameasina – Learning for Pacific Growth*, OECD.

OECD. 2008, *International Migration Outlook: 2008*, OECD, Paris.

Opara, O. 2018, "From settler society to working holiday heaven?: Patterns and issues of temporary labour migration to New Zealand", *New Zealand Sociology*, vol. 33, no. 1, pp. 29–52.

Overton, J. & Murray, W. 2013, "Class in a glass: Capital, neoliberalism and social space in the global wine industry", *Antipode*, vol. 45, no. 3, pp. 702–718.

PCF. 2013, *Annual Report of the Pacific Cooperation Foundation for the year ended 30 June 2013*, Pacific Cooperation Foundation, Wellington.

Petrou, K. & Connell, J. 2023a, *Pacific Islands guestworkers in Australia: The new blackbirds?* Springer Nature, Singapore.

Petrou, K. & Connell, J. 2023b, "Our 'Pacific family'. Heroes, guests, workers or a precariat?", *Australian Geographer*, vol. 54, no. 2, pp. 125–135.

PIFS. 2005a, *Forum communiqué Thirty-sixth Pacific Islands forum*, Pacific Islands Forum Secretariat, Madang.

PIFS. 2005b, *Summary record – remittances roundtable*, Pacific Island Forum Secretariat.

Piper, N. 2009, "The complex interconnections of the migration – development nexus: A social perspective", *Population, Space and Place*, vol. 15, no. 2, pp. 93–101.

Plant & Food Research. 2016, *Fresh facts 2015*, Horticulture New Zealand, Auckland.

Plimmer, N. 2006, *The future of the Pacific labour market: Labour mobility in the Pacific*, Pacific Cooperation Foundation, Wellington.

Rajkumar, D., Berkowitz, L., Vosko, L., Preston, V. & Latham, R. 2012, "At the temporary-permanent divide: How Canada produces temporariness and makes citizens through its security, work, and settlement policies", *Citizenship Studies*, vol. 16, no. 3–4, pp. 483–510.

Ramasamy, S., Vasantha, K., Bedford, R. & Bedford, C. 2008, "The Recognised Seasonal Employer policy: Seeking the elusive triple wins for development through international migration", *Pacific Economic Bulletin*, vol. 23, no. 3, pp. 171–186.

Rio, K. 2019, "The transformation of hierarchy following Christian conversion in Vanuatu", *Anthropological Forum*, vol. 29, no. 3, pp. 319–334.

Rio, K. & Eriksen, A. 2014, "A new man: The cosmological horizons of development, curses, and personhood in Vanuatu", in *Framing cosmologies: The anthropology of worlds*, eds. A. Abramson & M. Holbraad, Manchester University Press, Manchester, pp. 55–76.

Rockell, D. G. 2015, *Pacific Island labour programmes in New Zealand: An aid to Pacific Island development? A critical lens on the Recognised Seasonal Employer Policy*. Ph.D. thesis, Massey University.

Rohorua, H., Gibson, J., McKenzie, D. & Garcia Martinez, P. 2009, "How do Pacific island households and communities cope with seasonally absent members?", *Pacific Economic Bulletin*, vol. 24, no. 3, pp. 19–38.

Rose, N. 2000, "Community, citizenship, and the third way", *American Behavioral Scientist*, vol. 43, no. 9, pp. 1395–1411.

Rose, N. 1999, *Powers of freedom: Reframing political thought*, Cambridge University Press, Cambridge.

Rose, N. & Miller, P. 2010, "Political power beyond the State: Problematics of government", *British Journal of Sociology*, vol. 61, pp. 271–303.

Settlement Support New Zealand. 2011, *Recognised Seasonal Employer Get Ready DVD: Informesen blong ol wokman blong RSE*. New Zealand Department of Labour, Wellington.

Sharma, N. R. 2006, *Home economics: Nationalism and the making of 'migrant workers' in Canada*. University of Toronto Press, Toronto.

Sharpe, M. 2010, *Slave labour system rotten to the core*. Wellington, Stuff.co.nz.

Skeldon, R. 2010, "Managing migration for development: Is circular migration the answer", *Whitehead Journal of Diplomatic & International Relations*, vol. 11, pp. 21–33.

Slatter, C. 2006, "Neo-liberalism and the disciplining of Pacific Island States – the dual challenges of a global economic creed and a changed geopolitical order" in *Pacific futures*, ed. M. Powles, Pandanus Books, Research School of Pacific and Asian Studies, Australian National University, Canberra, pp. 91–110.

Smith, R. E. 2021, "The meaning of 'free' work: Service as a gift, and labor as a commodity for Ni-Vanuatu labor migrants" in *Work, society and the ethical self: Chimeras of freedom in the Neoliberal Era*, ed. C. Hann, Berghahn Books, New York, pp. 27–48.

Smith, R. E. 2019, "Be our guest/worker: Reciprocal dependency and expressions of hospitality in Ni-Vanuatu overseas labour migration", *Journal of the Royal Anthropological Institute*, vol. 25, no. 2, pp. 349–367.

Smith, R. E. 2018, "Changing standards of living: The paradoxes of building a good life in rural Vanuatu" in *The quest for the good life in precarious times: Informal, ethnographic perspectives on the domestic moral economy*, eds. C. Gregory & J. Altman, ANU Press, Canberra, pp. 33–55.

Smith, R. E. 2016, *Goal of the good house seasonal work and seeking a good life in Lamen and Lamen Bay, Epi, Vanuatu*. Ph.D. thesis, University of Manchester.

Stahl, C. & Appleyard, R. 2007, *Migration and development in the Pacific Islands: Lessons from the New Zealand experience*, Australian Agency for International Development, Canberra.

Stead, V. & Petrou, K., 2023, "Beyond the 'Triple Win': Pacific Islander farmworkers' use of social media to navigate labour mobility costs and possibilities through the COVID-19 pandemic", *Journal of Ethnic and Migration Studies*, vol. 49, no. 9, pp. 2194–2212.

Street, A. 2012, "Seen by the state: Bureaucracy, visibility and governmentality in a Papua New Guinean hospital", *Australian Journal of Anthropology*, vol. 23, no. 1, pp. 1–21.

Taylor, J. & Scarrow, S. 2010, "Seasonal Labour: An overview of the pilot Vakameasina project three months on ... Many benefits in project with RSE workers", *The Orchardist*, vol. 83, no. 2, pp. 42–44.

Tipples, R. & Rawlinson, P. 2014, *The RSE, a tool for dairying? Understanding the Recognised Seasonal Employer policy and its potential application to the dairy industry*, Working Paper no. 16, Faculty of Agribusiness & Commerce Lincoln University, Christchurch.

Truong, T. 2011, "The governmentality of transnational migration and security: The making of a New Subaltern" in *Transnational migration and human security: The migration-development-security nexus*, eds. T. Truong & D. Gasper, Springer, Berlin; New York, pp. 23–37.

Underhill-Sem, Y. & Marsters, E. 2017, *Labour mobility in the Pacific: A systematic literature review of development impacts*, New Zealand Institute for Pacific Research, Auckland.

Underhill-Sem, Y., Marsters, E., Bedford, R., Naidu, V. & Friesen, W. 2019, *Are there only winners? Labour mobility for sustainable development in the Pacific*, New Zealand Institute for Pacific Research, Auckland.

Vestergaard, J. 2009, *Discipline in the global economy? International finance and the end of liberalism*, Routledge, New York.

Voigt-Graf, C. 2006, "The potential social and development impacts of migration on Pacific Island countries" in *The future of the Pacific labour market: Labour mobility in the Pacific*, ed. N. Plimmer, Pacific Cooperation Foundation, Wellington, pp. 31–44.

Voigt-Graf, C. & Kanemasu, Y. 2019, *Labour mobility in Pacific Island countries*, International Labour Organisation Office for Pacific Island Countries, Suva.

Wainwright, E., Clements, Q., O'Callaghan, M. & Urwin, G. 2003, *Our failing neighbour Australia and the future of Solomon Islands*, Australian Strategic Policy Institute, Barton.

Wall, T. 2020, *Lockdown for profit: The puzzle and the problem of a growing migrant work scheme*, Hartevelt, J. ed, Wellington, Stuff.co.nz.

Wallis, J. 2012, "The Pacific: From 'arc of instability' to 'arc of responsibility' and then to 'arc of opportunity'?", *Security Challenges*, vol. 8, no. 4, pp. 1–12.

Ware, H. 2007, "Melanesian seasonal migration as a potential contribution to security", *Global Change, Peace & Security*, vol. 19, no. 3, pp. 221–242.

Ware, H. 2005, "Demography, migration and conflict in the Pacific", *Journal of Peace Research*, vol. 42, no. 4, pp. 435–454.

Ware, H. 2004, *Pacific instability and youth bulges: The devil in the demography and the economy*, Canberra, Australian Population Association 12th Biennial Conference Populations and Society: Issues, research, policy.

Webb, M., Marriott-Lloyd, P. & Grenfell, M. 2004, *Banning the bottle: Liquor bans in New Zealand*, Paper presented at the 3rd Australasian Drug Strategy Conference, Alice Springs, Australia.

Weiner, M. 1995, *The global migration crisis: Challenge to states and to human rights*. Harper Collins, New York.

Wesley-Smith, T. 2007, "The limits of self-determination in Oceania", *Social and Economic Studies*, vol. 56, no. 1, pp. 182–208.

Wesley-Smith, T. 1995, "Rethinking Pacific Islands studies", *Pacific Studies*, vol. 18, no. 2, pp. 115–137.

Whatman, R. & van Beek, J. 2008. "The seasonal labour strategy and the role of RSE in helping make transformative changes for employers and industry", *Labour, Employment and Work in New Zealand*, vol. 11, pp. 278–285.

Wickramasekara, P. 2011, *Circular Migration: A Triple Win or a Dead End*, Geneva, Global Union Research Network. Discussion Paper no. 15. http://dx.doi.org/10.2139/ssrn.1834762.

Wilson, M. A. 2014, "Precarious work – New Zealand experience", *New Zealand Journal of Employment Relations*, vol. 39, no. 2, pp. 22–33.

Wilson, P. & Fry, J. 2020, *Could do better: Migration and New Zealand's frontier firms*, NZ Institute of Economic Research, Auckland.

World Bank. 2006, *Pacific Islands at home and away: Expanding job opportunities for Pacific Islanders through labor mobility*. No. 37715-EAP. World Bank, Washington, DC.

World Bank. 2017, *Pacific possible: Long-term economic opportunities and challenges for Pacific. Island Countries*. World Bank, Washington, DC.

Yamamoto, T. S., Sunguya, B. F., Shiao, L. W. et al. 2012, "Migration of health workers in the Pacific Islands: A bottleneck to health development", *Asia Pacific Journal of Public Health*, vol. 24, no. 4, pp. 697–709.

Cambridge Elements

Global Development Studies

Peter Ho
Zhejiang University

Peter Ho is Distinguished Professor at Zhejiang University and high-level National Expert of China. He has held or holds the position of, amongst others, Research Professor at the London School of Economics and Political Science and the School of Oriental and African Studies, Full Professor at Leiden University and Director of the Modern East Asia Research Centre, Full Professor at Groningen University and Director of the Centre for Development Studies. Ho is well-cited and published in leading journals of development, planning and area studies. He published numerous books, including with *Cambridge University Press*, *Oxford University Press*, and *Wiley-Blackwell*. Ho achieved the William Kapp Prize, China Rural Development Award, and European Research Council Consolidator Grant. He chairs the International Conference on Agriculture and Rural Development (www.icardc.org) and sits on the boards of Land Use Policy, Conservation and Society, China Rural Economics, Journal of Peasant Studies, and other journals.

Servaas Storm
Delft University of Technology

Servaas Storm is a Dutch economist who has published widely on issues of macroeconomics, development, income distribution & economic growth, finance, and climate change. He is a Senior Lecturer at Delft University of Technology. He obtained a PhD in Economics (in 1992) from Erasmus University Rotterdam and worked as consultant for the ILO and UNCTAD. His latest book, co-authored with C.W.M. Naastepad, is *Macroeconomics Beyond the NAIRU* (Harvard University Press, 2012) and was awarded with the 2013 Myrdal Prize of the European Association for Evolutionary Political Economy. Servaas Storm is one of the editors of *Development and Change* (2006-now) and a member of the Institute for New Economic Thinking's Working Group on the Political Economy of Distribution.

Advisory Board
Arun Agrawal, *University of Michigan*
Jun Borras, *International Institute of Social Studies*
Daniel Bromley, *University of Wisconsin-Madison*
Jane Carruthers, *University of South Africa*
You-tien Hsing, *University of California, Berkeley*
Tamara Jacka, *Australian National University*

About the Series
The Cambridge Elements on Global Development Studies publishes ground-breaking, novel works that move beyond existing theories and methodologies of development in order to consider social change in real times and real spaces.

Cambridge Elements⹀

Global Development Studies

Elements in the Series

Temporary Migrants from Southeast Asia in Australia: Lost Opportunities
Juliet Pietsch

Mobile (for) Development: When Digital Giants Take Care of Poor Women
Marine Al Dahdah

Displacement in War-Torn Ukraine: State, Displacement and Belonging
Viktoriya Sereda

Investor States: Global Health at The End of Aid
Benjamin M. Hunter

Global Health Worker Migration: Problems and Solutions
Margaret Walton-Roberts

Going Public: The Unmaking and Remaking of Universal Healthcare
Ramya Kumar and Anne-Emanuelle Birn

The Problem of Private Health Insurance: Insights from Middle-Income Countries
Susan F. Murray

Development Subjectivities, Governmentality, and Migration Management in the Pacific
Lya Mainé Astonitas

A full series listing is available at: www.cambridge.org/EGDS

For EU product safety concerns, contact us at Calle de José Abascal, 56–1°, 28003 Madrid, Spain or eugpsr@cambridge.org.

www.ingramcontent.com/pod-product-compliance
Lightning Source LLC
LaVergne TN
LVHW020351260326
834688LV00045B/1656